COLD WAR WARRIOR

Rex Mangin

Books by Rex Mangin

Available as paperback and e-book

Infidelity Gun Running & Other Tales

Cold War Warrior

Flying The Pacific

Mercenary

Albert McConachie's Bad Day

Carrie Gray

Travel Bites

Introduction

A true story about a young lad who grew up in Blenheim, New Zealand, during the 1940s and early 50s. He developed an insatiable passion for flying, travelled to England and became a pilot in the Royal Air Force. He soon found himself involved in the United Kingdom's nuclear testing programme in the Pacific. This took him around the world and in just a few short years he found himself on the front line of the Cold War in Germany.

If things had turned ugly this young Kiwi, along with others, was going to unleash nuclear mayhem on Europe and would no doubt have perished in the process. This is his story.

HARRY

Gone Too Soon

Contents

Foreword

On the 24th of May 2007 Harry Scarff passed away. Harry was my close friend during that early part of my life when I found myself caught up in the Cold War. Just twelve days before his unexpected death we had met up again at a reunion in England after a gap of forty-five years. A few days after his death Harry's son asked me about an old engraved copper tankard he had come across amongst his father's possessions, he wondered if I might know anything about it, yes indeed, I knew all about it. It was this inquiry from Harry's son that caused me to reflect on that early part of my life and the things I had done. I decided it was all worth recording and thus the idea of writing this story was born. The tale about the tankard appears towards the end, it's a significant link with the past.

Early Days

'Ok Harry, here we go.' I nosed the big Canberra over and headed for the ground in a steep dive, at about 600 feet with the target firmly in the gun sight I squeezed the trigger. Four 20mm Hispano cannons burst into life and sent a shudder through the aircraft, I could see the shells shredding the canvas target on the ground. When we were ridiculously close I stopped firing, pulled up hard, and climbed away. Harry, my navigator, was jammed up in the nose cone, he must have been terrified; Again! We were at a live firing range in the old West Germany practising air to ground gunnery, I was having a ball, Harry was not! How did I come to be doing this?

Well I was a front line jet jock in the Royal Air Force, actually I was in NATO's Second Tactical Air Force in Germany, how did I get to be there? it's a long story.

In our cottage on a beach in Auckland New Zealand amongst all the wine glasses there's a copper tankard, it's lined with silver and looks old and tarnished. There are some words engraved on it. *IN HAZY MEMORY OF SALISBURY SOUTHERN RHODESIA JUNE 1962.* On closer inspection the engraving is a bit rough, the Os look like Ds however the quality of the copper and the silver lining appears to be surprisingly good. This tankard is a constant reminder to me about the early part of my life, the part that now seems so very far away when I was involved in the Cold War in Europe. On occasions I ask myself, did all that really happen?

Was that me thundering around Germany in a jet, right down on the deck, eyeballing the East Germans? Was it me out in the Libyan desert amongst the flies, the sand, the heat and the sweat, trying to toss a bomb onto a target from very low level? Did I really shoot up the Larnaca range out in Cyprus with those big 20mm cannons? Did I really fly around those Norwegian Fjords in all that murk, ice and snow? That gun running business in Tunisia, did that actually happen? Was that me flying over the vastness of East Africa, the endless deserts of the Sudan? Did I do that sabre-rattling for Queen and Country in Central Africa? Was I really involved in that nuclear testing in the Pacific in the 1950s? Did I really wander around East Berlin at the height of the Cold War? Yes I did, it was all part of my Big OE, let me explain.

I came into this world way back in 1936 in Wellington, a second son for my hard-working parents. It was not long after the great depression, times were tough. While I was still young the family moved to Blenheim where my father found work as a farm manager on a series of dairy farms around Blenheim. I have pleasant memories from those early years one place in particular, White's Farm.

The house was old and run down, the farmyard animals had taken to wandering inside. I thought this was pretty neat, a sheep or a pig rummaging around in the kitchen. The hens, we called them chooks, were constantly wandering about inside, and pooing. One day my father suggested I might like to help him build a culvert under the dirt track that led up to the house. It was down by the main road where the track to the farm branched off, the culvert was just a large water pipe under the dirt track. This was great, I was really helping Dad, we were building this huge bridge, I was about six at the time. The culvert is still there. I have gone out of my way in recent years when visiting Blenheim to drive by and have a look.

Aunty Mary, Mum's sister, lived in Havelock, a small town at the head of the Pelorus Sound. The Marlborough Sounds are a series of flooded valleys, a prominent feature at the top of New Zealand's

South Island. Havelock's not far from Blenheim, it was popular with us and we spent a lot of time there. These days the Sounds are a big tourist attraction however during my childhood the place was a real backwater. Mary's house was a big wooden place that Uncle Doug had built with Kauri timber he had milled himself just after they married. There was a small clay bank down the front by the main road covered with ivy and the place was called Ivy Bank. They had two girls, Molly and Ivy. My older brother Noel and myself had a lot of fun with the girls when we went to Havelock which was pretty often. There was a downside to visiting however, the road from Blenheim was not sealed, it was dusty and rough. The Newmans bus, which was the only way of getting there, was a real 'dunga,' smelly exhaust fumes, no springs, well it certainly felt like that, and the dust just poured in, real choking stuff, I always felt sick after a trip on that awful bus, it was a real 'put off.' A big mulberry tree dominated the back yard, a favourite place, up the mulberry tree eating mulberries which always resulted in red stains on our clothes.

Life at Mary's was real pioneering stuff, no electricity, the fridge was a muslin covered box hanging in a tree, 'Daisy' the cow supplied the milk, Mary separated out the butterfat then made butter in a churn. Uncle Doug made frequent trips into the thick bush up the hill behind the house and shot wild pigs. He butchered them and produced all sorts of nice things, bacon, smoked pork, salted pork, pork sausages. The meat was dark and tasty, pig fern, their main food source, gave it the dark colour. Opening off Mary's big kitchen was a room where Doug hung pieces of pork to dry, it gave the room a distinctive smell. Mary's kitchen featured a large black Shacklock wood burning stove, it was always going, day and night. Like most housewives of that era she was an excellent cook, sponge cakes to die for, cheese biscuits, pikelets, lots of very tasty things. There was a telephone on the kitchen wall, a large wooden affair with a crank handle on one side, a big hand piece on the other, a party line. Every now and again the phone would make some ringing noises, the idea was to identify which ringing sequence was meant for you and not one of the other six addressees on the same line, it was a pretty modern gadget. Molly and Ivy had become adept at listening to other people's conversations without being detected.

My older brother, Noel, was a foody, he had discovered that the creek running through Mary's garden was home to a lot of crawlers or Koura as they are called, a small freshwater crayfish native to New Zealand, excellent eating. Noel would spend hours splashing around in this creek chasing these things and he always finished up with quite a haul, he would cook them up in the kitchen then eat the lot. The creek held cockabullies as well, a small freshwater fish, Noel would catch these as well, not sure what he used them for, but he was always catching them.

There was one thing about Aunty Mary's place that was not so good, the toilet, an outhouse well away from the main house, it smelt, actually it stank. There was no sewerage system so Uncle Doug had built this outhouse up by the orchard. Inside there was a seat with a hole in it and a large bin underneath. When the bin was full, or the smell became unbearable, Doug would pull this repulsive thing out and bury the contents, dreadful business. A nighttime visit to the toilet was not a pleasant experience, something to be avoided. The outhouse was full of spiders, big spiders and there would always be possums and hedgehogs moving about making strange noises and it always seemed to be raining whenever you wanted to go in fact going to the toilet during the night could be quite an ordeal for a young fellow.

Another thing fixed in my memory from those early days at Mary's, the 'rattly bridges.' Out in front of Havelock was a large swamp, it formed the top end of Pelorus Sound, the road across this swamp included two wooden bridges, they made a distinctive rattle whenever a vehicle drove across. Lying in bed on a still night, not a sound to be heard, rattle rattle rattle, silence, then rattle rattle rattle; slow, fast, speeding, how long between rattles. They're long gone, concrete now, no character.

Access to the Sounds was by water only, no roads. A mail boat serviced Pelorus Sound three times a week. A trip on the mail boat, a fifty-foot launch, was a real thrill, I must have done it dozens of times. Another highlight was the annual family camping trip somewhere in the sounds. We had this huge war surplus army tent. Every Christmas we would load the tent and all our gear onto the mail boat and get dropped off at some idyllic bay way down the Pelorus, 'pick us up in ten days time.' The fishing was excellent, plenty of blue cod. We lived off the land during those camping holidays, lived very well too.

At some stage during my childhood I became infatuated with aeroplanes, I think it must have been all the flying activity around Blenheim that brought it about. It was wartime, there was a big flying school at a nearby airfield, RNZAF Woodbourne. White's Farm was not far from this airfield and one day when I came home from school there was an aeroplane in the back yard, well not quite. A Vickers Vildebeest, a big biplane the Air Force used for pilot training, had made a forced landing in the back paddock and finished up quite close to the house, I thought this was just the greatest thing in the world. It became even more incredible when the men came from Woodbourne, took the wings off and carted the whole plane away.

When I was ten Dad gave up farm management, bought a shoe shop in Blenheim and we moved into town, 12 Grady Street, right next to the racecourse and close to Lansdown Park, the local rugby field. Farming had been difficult in the Wairau valley, poor farms, stony ground, burnt brown paddocks, the land would not support enough sheep or cattle to make farming viable, land values were rock bottom, who would want to farm in Marlborough?

When we moved into town I joined the Cubs, then the Boy Scouts. The Scouting movement was very active in Blenheim and during the next few years I got to enjoy plenty of camping. At every opportunity the Scouts were off camping in the foothills around the Wairau valley. I soon became conversant with all those skills that the Scouting movement teaches. These abilities were to come in handy. One of the junior Scout masters was a rather irresponsible character always finding fun ways of doing things, I did notice this chap was never allowed to be in sole charge, always 'number two.' On one occasion when we were camping he showed us his sure fire method of fresh water fishing, he lit the fuse on a stick of gelignite, a powerful explosive used for log splitting, and tossed it into the local stream. When all the water, debris, and what have you, had settled he showed us how you just gathered up all the eels, trout, koura, cockabullies, etc, you wanted, easy, they were all floating belly up in the water. As I mentioned this fellow was a bit irresponsible but he certainly had some bright ideas. I enjoyed my time with the Scouts in Blenheim.

Getting around meant pedalling a bike, cars were a rarity, expensive, and just not available. Biking, although not appreciated at the time, was one of the best things that could have happened to us, it made us fit, strong and healthy, qualities that set us up for life. As youngsters we did not quite see it that way especially when pedalling home from school into a strong nor'wester on a wet day. The family never did own a car, we all rode bikes, it was the norm for just about everyone in Blenheim.

What about a driving licence? a young fellow had to have one of those, not much opportunity to use it, but you had to have one. An older acquaintance of mine had a mate who owned an old Chevrolet pick up, 'what are my chances?' 'Yep, good, this is how the truck works, off you go.' I was sixteen at the time, I taught myself. Crash gearbox, fortunately a very rugged gearbox, some scary moments, a bit of advice here and there, and I could drive, or so I thought. I presented myself to the local Traffic Officer who was well aware of my driving efforts, Blenheim was very 'small town.' The driving test developed into a driving lesson; at the end of it I was given a licence; just!

Lansdown Park, the local rugby field, just along the road from home. The main ground had a large scoreboard on a bank at one end that was manually operated, it was not long before I got myself the job operating it on Saturday afternoons. I would sit up in the box behind the board taking a very close interest in the game and altering the large scoring figures being displayed on the board immediately there was a change, there was no room for error, a mistake with the score would bring an immediate and very vocal response from the crowd. I became interested in rugby and started playing for the school team where I progressed through the ranks eventually finished up in the first fifteen. I have been an avid rugby fan ever since.

My father's hobby was caged birds, apparently this interest had been with him since childhood. Wherever we lived there would always be some sort of aviary where Dad would keep budgies. He entered them in competitions around the country and was always winning lots of certificates and trophies. When we moved to Grady Street he built a really big aviary with a separate breeding room and became really serious about his budgies. His knowledge and skill must have been recognised nationally because he became a caged bird show judge and travelled all over New Zealand judging.

Not long after the move to Grady Street I became interested in shooting, my father decided this would be a good sport for me and he would give a helping hand. There were a lot of rabbits around Blenheim, we decided to go after them. I was still young, far too young to have a rifle so Dad became my minder. We would pedal our bikes out to a stony riverbed near Blenheim and Dad would

The Rabbit Shooter

supervise while I shot rabbits with a single shot Remington .22 rifle. This riverbed was home to thousands of rabbits, they were a real pest. The idea was to head shoot them so the skin would be intact and the body meat unspoilt. All these rabbits would be running around the riverbed, every now and again they would all stop, sit up, and listen. This was the time, careful aim, bang, one shot only and it must be a headshot. The rabbits would take off at the sound of the shot. About twenty seconds later they would all stop, sit up and listen again. This gave me time to reload the single shot Remington, bang, another rabbit. Ten or so rabbits we would call it a day and pedal our bikes back home. I skinned them and strung the skins on wire frames to dry, a couple of weeks later I sold the skins to the local dealer. The bodies were gutted, cleaned up and Mum would cook them, delicious. It would be rabbit stew, baked rabbit, or rabbit pie, for a few days. If the rabbit was body shot then the skin had no value because there was a hole in it and the meat would be a mess. The rabbit shooting went on for several years. I became a very good shot with that old Remington. This ability to shoot was spotted at school where there was a long-standing tradition of Marlborough College winning all the National shooting competitions. There was the Weekly Press competition and The Islington Cup for small bore and the Earl Roberts competition for 303s. I was conscripted into all these teams where I remained a fixture for all my years at Marlborough College. We just kept winning year in year out, I still have all the medals and cups to show for it. On a couple of occasions I managed to score 101 out of 100, excuse me? Well in shooting if you clip the inner ring, it's a bull, 10 points, if the hole is entirely within the inner ring, it's 10.1, not an easy thing to do. In a few years time this ability to shoot was to prove invaluable when I got to shoot seriously big guns from aeroplanes. I was able to put my shooting skills to good use while still at school, shooting Possums. We were still frequent visitors to Mary's place. Her orchard produced a lot of apples pears and peaches but was plagued with Possums, they destroyed everything. The bush behind the house was home to hundreds, probably thousands of them, they ate every bit of fruit that appeared on the orchard trees. Uncle Doug had given up shooting them it was a no win situation however now that I was a bit older I took a big interest in Possum shooting. I made a crude spotlight using a car headlamp and a small motorbike battery, the light was strapped on my head, the battery on my back. The trusty single shot Remington was used and nighttime Possum shooting became popular. Into the orchard around ten o'clock, move your head around until you picked up two orange reflections in the spotlight close together, Possum's eyes, it did not take long to spot them, they were everywhere, aim between the two orange bits, bang one Possum, reload, do it again, there was just an endless supply of the things. After a while it got a bit boring, there was no market for the skins, the meat, well you would not want to eat it; shooting Possums was just too easy. Over a couple of years I must have shot hundreds, it did not make the slightest difference to their numbers, it was still hard to get any fruit from Mary's orchard. I remember Mum getting a bit hostile about the holes in my shirts, the old motorbike battery would slop a bit of acid about, not the best for a shirt.

I must have been about eleven when I took to making model aeroplanes, it developed into a real obsession. I was making all sorts of planes, all flying ones. In 1953 the National Model Aeroplane Championships were held in Blenheim at Omaka aerodrome. I entered my aeroplanes in many of the events and managed to become the NZ National Junior Champion. There was a competition for model gliders included in these events the idea being to select a New Zealand team to represent the country at an international glider competition in Europe. I won this event, I could not believe my luck. It was not to be however, the team never got to go to Europe. My interest in model aeroplanes continued right up until I left home. I have often had a hankering to take up this hobby again, it's not happened yet, but you never know.

Mum was a keen gardener, she planted a grapevine that

eventually grew right across the back of our house at Grady Street. Mum would prune it and do all the things that were required. This vine really flourished, it produced magnificent grapes. We used to sit out the back and eat them directly off the vine. The only downside were the blackbirds, they liked Mum's grapes as well so it was a bit of a scramble to get the good grapes first. I did have a slug gun at the time so that evened things up a little. The significance of the extraordinary success of Mum's grapevine was, I'm afraid, lost on us at the time. Today the Wairau Valley is New Zealand's, probably the world's, premier white wine producing area and the price of that stony land that Dad had so much trouble trying to make a living from? I can only guess!

A point of interest here. Those of you who are wine buffs may have sampled a range of whites carrying the Stoneleigh label. This vineyard is established on the very riverbed where we used to shoot rabbits all those years ago. I have visited the place in recent times and asked if there were any rabbits around. 'Yes, indeed there are, in fact they are a problem, they eat the new growth on the vines,' 'really, what you need is someone to shoot them;' now there's a thought.

I still have relatives in Marlborough so we get to go there quite often, what a difference. My childhood memories of burnt brown paddocks, the sun beating down, sunburn, a few scrawny sheep, some miserable looking cows, plenty of nodding thistle, worthless stony land, lots of rabbits, old gum trees and Mum's grapevine that did so well. There was a message there, we missed it! Today the Wairau valley is a very different scene, lush vineyards as far as the eye can see, magnificent wineries, restaurants, not a sheep or a cow in sight and apparently still some rabbits. Some things change, some things remain the same.

My older brother, Noel, had a good singing voice, he was very interested in music, particularly classical in all its forms. Mum was rather proud of this and encouraged him to develop this singing ability which he did, he developed into quite an exceptional boy soprano. He was very successful in numerous music competitions and eventually moved on to a full-time career in music becoming a well-known opera singer in Europe. Noel was five years my senior, we were not close, we certainly had widely differing interests. I must have been about fifteen when Noel left home and moved to Auckland to advance his singing career, I saw very little of him after that. Noel's ability to sing had a direct impact on my own life in those early days. As I mentioned he was five years my senior and well known around Blenheim for his singing. When I came along it was assumed that I too could sing, not my thing, but the pressure was on, Mum pushed it, a bit too hard, I rebelled. I did have a singing voice of sorts and I found myself in the church choir. The Anglican Church in Alfred Street in Blenheim had a choir, I was a reluctant member of it for several years.

My obsession with aeroplanes manifested itself in numerous ways, I decided I wanted to make a career in aviation, the desire to become a pilot did not surface until later. I had been making inquiries about what was available in the aviation world then one day while visiting some relatives in Wellington, I must have been about fifteen at the time, I went out to Rongotai, an airfield near Wellington, The de Havilland Aircraft Company had a facility there. I fronted up to their hanger and made inquiries about what I needed to do to get into aviation. An elderly fellow advised me to go back to school, continue my education, then seriously consider joining the Air Force.

On another occasion I sought out the man who had been instrumental in starting up an airfreight operation in Blenheim, Straits Air Freight Express, Bob Hamilton. He had a fatherly talk to me about aviation in general and again advised me the place to learn the business was the Air Force. I was in the college Air Training

Corps and the local Blenheim Air Training Core as well. This gave me access to all sorts of aviation activities, Air Force visits, air shows, access to visiting military aircraft and lots more, all incredibly interesting to a young lad. Around this time I realised I wanted to fly aeroplanes. I started saving my pennies with a view to taking flying lessons at the local aero club. Mum did not like this idea, 'a pilot, you should think about a real career.' Dad did not say too much. I stayed at school and did reasonably well, school certificate, university entrance, higher leaving certificate, but bursaries and university did not interest me, I had decided I wanted to be a pilot. Poor Mum, 'I think you should consider architecture, or surveying, you are not going to be a pilot.' Bit like red rag to a bull, 'I am going to be a pilot Mum, and I am going to be a pilot in the Royal Air Force in England.' 'Heaven forbid, you ungrateful boy and after all we have done for you,' Dad still did not say too much. Poor Mum, she just would not accept that I wanted to fly aeroplanes. 'Well Mum, I have applied to the Air Force for pilot training.' I was seventeen, things were a bit tense at home. Fate threw Mum a lifeline, I got knocked back by the Air Force, no real reason, there were so many applicants they had to reduce the numbers. Mum was happy, 'there now, what about architecture?' 'Not a chance Mum, I am going to fly.' I applied again and this time I was going to succeed, *I had decided.* I was successful and found myself on number twenty combined aircrew course at RNZAF Taieri near Dunedin starting at the beginning of May. It was 1955, I was 18 years old and I was in, little did I know just what I was in for. The Air Force was very picky about just who graduated from a wings course, the failure rate was frightening. Achieving was not enough, you had to achieve at a required rate, the learning curve was steep. I left home, and Blenheim, one sunny morning in May 1955 on a Newmans bus for Christchurch, it was to be my last happy memory of Blenheim. At that time there was a scheme in existence whereby a young lad in New Zealand could apply to become a pilot in the Royal Air Force in England, this was the scheme under which I had joined. To be successful you had to join the RNZAF and survive their initial wings training. You did not actually get your wings with the RNZAF because the RAF required all new pilots to be jet qualified, the RNZAF did not have any jet training aircraft in 1955. Interestingly, now more than sixty years on, the RNZAF still does not have any jet training aircraft. If you survived this initial stage that went on for eight months and the powers that be decided you had *'the right stuff,'* and you were not likely to fail further along the line then you travelled to England and continued with jet training in the RAF.

The New Zealand training started on Tiger Moths at Taieri, it was wintertime, snow on the ground. It was like something you see in the movies, early morning runs through the snow, drill sergeants barking at you on the parade ground, inspections, spit and polish, lots of study, and the best part, we were taught to fly a Tiger Moth. Now for those readers who are not aviation buffs let me tell you about a Tiger Moth. It's a small biplane, made by The de Havilland Aircraft Company, it dates from the 1930s, an old design and a good one. They were produced in their thousands, an excellent aeroplane to learn to fly on. The ones at Taieri were quite old, left overs from the war years. We were to spend three months at Taieri, I was just lapping it up, right in my element, it did not last. You may have picked up on the fact that my father and I were close, we did a lot of things together, particularly when I was very young. One day, while I was at Taieri, I was called in by the Commanding Officer who told me he had received a phone call from my mother advising that my father had been diagnosed with terminal cancer, he had been given six months to live, I was completely devastated, my father was a pillar of strength in my life. I was offered the chance to terminate my training and return home to be with my mother, what should I do?

Going home would probably mean the end of my flying ambitions, it was a testing time. I phoned Mum, her wish was for me to remain at Taieri, that is what Dad would want. She had accepted the reality that all I wanted to do with my life was fly aeroplanes, so that's what happened, I stayed in the Air Force. My remaining time at Taieri was

Tiger Moth

miserable, I enjoyed learning to fly but emotionally I was a mess. I immersed myself in all the learning that was required, I found that this occupied my mind and stopped me from thinking too much about my father. There was a surprise benefit from this, I scored the top academic marks and managed to top the course overall; I was awarded the Brevet Club Trophy, a large silver cup. Perhaps this could be construed as a gift from Dad.

When we moved to Wigram, near Christchurch, for the advanced flying training on Harvards things got really tough, Dad deteriorated, I was called home on two occasions. Dad passed away suddenly in

December 1955, I was not there. I returned home from Wigram immediately, the Air Force supplied a Harvard and my instructor flew me to Woodbourne, it really hurt not being there when Dad died. The funeral was just before Christmas, I don't think I have ever been so miserable in all my life. I had just turned nineteen.

The Wigram course was tough, the required standard was high, so was the failure rate. Fridays were 'chop days' when those who had failed to make the grade during that week were advised of their failure, they were required to depart from Wigram that evening. On Friday evenings we would go along to Christchurch railway station and farewell those unlucky souls, we all dreaded Fridays. On the positive side, the flying was great, the Harvard was a serious aeroplane and flying it was exhilarating, I certainly needed something good to be happening in my life. I guess I must have got lucky because I survived the course. In January 1956 I boarded the SS Rangitane in Wellington harbour for a four-week journey to England, I had just turned 19 and had 112 flying hours in my logbook, Mum was distraught. I had a mate, Peter Dwyer from Christchurch, he had joined under the same scheme as myself, we had been on the same course at Taieri and Wigram. There were three others fellows who wanted in on the RAF scheme, they had fallen by the wayside.

It was a sad departure for me, Dad had died just three weeks earlier, I was really hurting.

Off To England

Peter Dwyer and myself sailed out of Wellington harbour on a fine summer's day leaving a sad faced bunch of relatives behind on the wharf. It would be five long years before we would see them again, I think they thought they might never see us again. We were leaving behind a lifestyle, which although we did not appreciate it at the time, had equipped us extremely well for what lay ahead, we were about to find out that life outside New Zealand was very different to what we were used to. The trip to England was meant to take four weeks but the boat broke down, it took six. The contract we had with the RAF was a twelve-year commission as a pilot with the option of leaving after eight, a free trip back to New Zealand for two months leave on completion of five years service, and a free return to New Zealand on completion of the contract. We held the rank of Acting Pilot Officer. As we were Officers we were allocated suitable accommodation on the boat, single cabins on the top deck, *how lucky can you get*. The Rangitane was operated by the NZ Shipping Company, it was a dual-purpose ship that carried both freight and passengers. Chilled and frozen NZ lamb and 250 passengers, about 150 of these were youngsters off on the Big OE, the Overseas Experience, a right of passage for young people at that time. In 1955 it really was an OE, it took four weeks just to get to Europe, no big jets, you had to go by boat. About half of the OEers were girls in six-berth accommodation way down in the bilges. It was to be a memorable trip!

The first couple of days were a settling in period where we got to know our fellow travellers. The evening dining was done in two sittings, one of them formal. As we were RAF Officers it was the formal sitting for us. We were placed at a table for four, the other two were a couple of girls from Christchurch. Small world, we had noticed these very same girls a couple of months earlier at a restaurant in Christchurch. They had come to our attention because they were enjoying a fairly noisy going away dinner with some of their friends, we just happened to be in the same restaurant. They were characters, always an eye on 'the main chance.' They quickly determined we were not wealthy lads, a bit young as well so they devoted a lot of effort trying to catch the attention of those males they thought might be a better bet. Peter and I wondered how long it would be before they 'moved up' in the dinner table stakes but it didn't happen; they did score an early invitation to the Captain's table for dinner though, we had to wait about ten days for ours. It took all of the first week for them to decide we were actually a couple of nice fellows, no money, but nice, they stayed at our table for the duration of the trip.

First call, Pitcairn Island. The locals came out in their longboats to sell their wares, I was blown away by the appearance of these people. They were all descendants from the Bounty mutineers, Christians, McCoys, Mills, Youngs, Smiths and the rest. Their gene pool had not been refreshed for many generations, the inbreeding was obvious, small mongoloid looking people. We offloaded supplies into their longboats the design of which had not changed from the original Bounty design, and continued on our way.

We had teamed up with some Kiwis and some Australians, boys and girls. They were a bit older than us, we were the youngsters on board, *and in those single cabins on the top deck!* We involved ourselves in all the onboard activities as a group, it did not include our two dinner partners however, they were playing a different game. All the usual things were available, deck tennis, quoits, shuffleboard, bingo, various pool games and of course a lot of activity at the numerous bars. There was a fair bit of 'girl chasing' going on as well, we found ourselves having a really good time.

One evening approaching the Panama Canal there was a loud bang, the ship shuddered and slowed right down, what was that? 'That' was one of the ship's two engines having a catastrophic failure, interesting, what happens now? Two days in Panama while the damage was assessed, Panama City, pretty exotic place for a young lad from New Zealand. When we berthed in Panama some American Marines from the local garrison came aboard and struck up an instant friendship with our group; they offered to show us around the city later in the day when they came off duty. Their generous offer was double edged, they were interested in our girls. We did not have a problem with that, the Americans seemed to be nice guys, the girls thought so as well. We arranged to meet with a couple of them later in the day. This was a good idea, we were way out of our comfort zone here. The Americans were indeed good company and yes they did make a play for the girls. They showed us around Panama City, took us to places I will not be telling mother about. It was an interesting night, an eye opener for a naïve young lad from the back blocks. I will never forget that night out in Panama City it made a huge impression on my young mind.

Our damaged engine turned into a real problem, it could not be fixed at Panama, we would have to go to Colon at the eastern end of the canal for further assessment. The journey through the canal was incredible, a bit different to the Opawa river back in Blenheim. The actual waterway across the isthmus consists of a couple of sections of man-made canal and a large lake, Gatun. There are two locks where ships are raised to the level of the lake. At the eastern end there's another section of canal and another lock that lowers the ships down to the level of the Caribbean ocean. Everywhere there were ships, every size, shape and colour imaginable, it was a very busy place, the surrounding jungle made it hot and humid. I found myself mesmerised by the sight of it all and spent hours at the ships rail just taking it all in. A day in Colon, the answer, the engine could not be fixed there either, it required dry-docking, the verdict, continue on to England on one engine at reduced speed. We sailed out through the Caribbean then out across the Atlantic at a very reduced speed. 'We're going to be late for our wings course Pete.' We were late, a bit too late, we would have to wait for the start of the next course.

Our slow progress had some curious side effects. An extra two weeks at sea had not been catered for. No problem in the dining room, I did not notice any decline in the standard, but the various bars started to run short, no more tonic, sorry girls. The ultimate disaster was announced as we sailed up the English Channel, there's no more beer. We were twenty-four hours from berthing in England.

I have vivid memories from sailing up the Channel in early March 1956, all those vapour trails in the sky, I had never seen that before. They were twisting and turning and every now and again there would be a sonic boom. This was the RAF, and the American Air Force, doing what they did, over the Channel. The RAF had Hawker Hunter jet fighters, lots of them, these were some of the planes we were seeing. Our enthusiasm was boundless, that will be us soon Pete, imagine!

The Rangitane limped past Southampton, the original destination, and continued on to Tilbury where we docked. Bleak, cold, and foggy when we finally arrived. We disembarked and spent a couple of hours mucking around finding our suitcases and being processed by officialdom, it was all a bit depressing. Then we travelled up to London by train, I was unimpressed by the drab foggy countryside. At a huge grubby railway station in London we said fond goodbyes to all our shipboard friends then the Royal Air Force grabbed us, bundled us into the back of a small van with all our worldly possessions and off we went to the Air Ministry where we were quite literally dumped, with all our gear, on the front steps, welcome to England.

It got worse. We lugged all our gear inside, into a small room, where we spent the rest of the day waiting around. Numerous people came to talk to us, the tone of their conversations was not encouraging. 'Oh, you are the two New Zealanders who have arrived late on the slow boat, not sure what we will do with you,' all very encouraging. At five pm we were still holed up in this cold room when someone realized that we would require a bed for the night. It was suggested that we might catch the tube out to Hendon where they could probably accommodate us for the night. 'What's the tube? and where is Hendon?' 'Oh!' We were bundled back into the van with all our possessions and driven to Hendon, which turned out to be a very old RAF Station on the edge of London. We were fed up, this was becoming a nightmare. Hendon was a pleasant surprise, we stopped at what appeared to be an old English country house, the Officers Mess. Again we found ourselves on the front steps with all our luggage. A keen young chap introduced himself and took us inside, 'I will show you your accommodation.' The place appeared to be very comfortable, big log fire, large lounge, big dining room, couple of large bars, warm and friendly atmosphere, looks pretty good. We continued on through the mess, out the back door, across a muddy patch of ground, and into a drab little annex, 'sorry chaps the mess is full at the moment so this will be your accommodation.'

We remained at Hendon while higher authority pondered what to do with these two Kiwis who had turned up late, not a good start. We had been scheduled for a jet Provost course at RAF Hullavington, we had missed the start of that course by a week. We were now rescheduled for the next one starting in five weeks, five weeks! It looked like we had a lot of time to kill. Peter and I decided to see the sights of London. We did the lot, all those things that good tourists do, Westminster Abby, trip on the Thames, changing of the guard at the Palace, Hyde Park Corner on a Sunday, Tower of London. It was there that I traced a distant relative, a Lord Lovat who got offside with the establishment and lost his head. It was all so interesting, and the pubs, nothing like that in New Zealand. One place that made an impression was an old pub on the Thames riverbank called The Prospect of Whitby. It was extremely old, and famous, ex-pats from the colonies had made it their regular. We went along there quite a few times during that first couple of weeks and met some of the folk off the Rangitane. One evening we had to console one of the ships officers. This chap, a likeable Scott, was an engineering officer, he had taken up with a New Zealand girl during the trip. They were both in the Prospect one evening very despondent, he had just been fired. When the engine failure had occurred approaching Panama it had also knocked out part of the ships refrigeration system. It had been his job to get onto this and jury-rig the system so it would continue working. I guess he had been preoccupied at the time, after all she was a gorgeous girl. When the chillers were opened at Tilbury a lot of the lamb had turned green, responsibility for this had been laid on him.

Scrumpy was the drink of choice at the Prospect, apple cider, it was strong stuff, bit too strong for a young lad from the colonies. I remember stumbling out of the place on several occasions and heading off through the tall dockside warehouses to the local tube station. In recent years I've been back, the Prospect's still there, full of continental tourists who arrive in buses and stay five minutes, no scrumpy!

One day a fellow in the mess asked if we would like to fly in an Anson aircraft to London Airport, we could see what it was like flying in the UK, would we what! Off we went, landed at Heathrow, took off again and returned to Hendon. I did not see a thing, the murkiest flying conditions I had ever encountered in my short flying career. Hmm, flying in the UK might be a bit different to a Canterbury nor'wester at Wigram.

It was about week three, we were right into our sightseeing, really enjoying ourselves when we were told there had been a change of plan, we were now going to RAF Feltwell in Norfolk to do an initial flying training course on piston Provosts. Hang on we've done that in New Zealand, we're here to do the jet part of the wings course. Well chaps that's not going to happen, you will do a complete RAF wings course and you will start on piston aircraft, and oh, by the way, you are to be at Feltwell by tomorrow evening. The next morning it was the little van again, this time it dumped us at Hendon station, onto a train with all our gear, into the centre of London, out of the train, into a taxi, across London to another station where we loaded all our gear onto a trolley that we trundled around this huge station until we found our next train where we loaded it all on board again. Out again in the wilds of Norfolk, into another taxi and finally there we were on the front steps of the Junior Officers Mess at RAF Feltwell surrounded by all our gear on a cold wet afternoon. I was close to tears. One day I will be a jet jock, I just know this!

We spent the next five months at Feltwell flying piston engined Provosts, the basic RAF training aeroplane of the day. This was not supposed to be happening, we had done it all back in New Zealand on Harvards, we were supposed to be doing the advanced jet stage leading up to RAF wings. It's going to be a long time before we get our wings Pete but we'll certainly be well trained. The Provost flying was a repeat of what we had already done in New Zealand, this gave us a huge advantage over the English lads who were on the same course. There were various competitions along the way, aerobatics, navigation tests, landing competitions, we took all the prizes, well what did they expect, we had done it all before. Some realities about life in England became apparent during this period. One day Peter and I were having a meal in the mess when we were approached by a fellow who was on a course one ahead of ours, he asked us to move to another table, pardon me? 'Well you are sitting at the senior students table, you are juniors, your table is down there,' we had just run into the English class system. Another thing, no pumpkin, I had been brought up on pumpkin, I really liked it. 'Pig food, you colonials have no class,' *well really*, I could see it was not going to be all straight forward with these English lads. The tables were turned a couple of weeks later when our course, and the one ahead of us, went off to the local indoor swimming pool for emergency procedures training, that's where we learnt all about coming down in the sea and getting into life rafts. The pool was a good one, Peter and I dived in and swam a couple of lengths, the English lads all remained on the side of the pool. 'Come on you guys, jump in, it's lovely,' nobody moved. The penny dropped, none of them could swim. This threw me, 'what do you mean you can't swim?' We came from a society where it was assumed you could swim, I cannot recall a kid in New Zealand not being able to swim. In England it's different, it was quite common not to be able to swim. Sweet revenge offered itself when I noticed our 'senior friend' from the dining room standing on the side of the pool. 'Come on jump in' I ventured, 'I'll mother you, make sure you don't drown.' Other things became apparent like the food. Coming from New Zealand we were used to eating excellent food, something I had taken for granted all my life, the rest of the world however does not necessarily eat as well as the colonials in New Zealand. The food in the mess at Feltwell was a real shock, it was awful, elsewhere it was not much better, the food seemed to lack taste. There were no milkshakes, what's a milkshake? no meat pies as we knew them, no Kiwi style sausages and everything seemed to have been cooked in a frying pan, the beer was warm as well. 'Pete, I guess we will just have to adapt.' We did adapt to the English way and we made them familiar with some of our colonial ways as well. The English lads were a good lot, lifelong friendships were made at Feltwell.

Next to the airfield was Feltwell village and a very old pub, the

Oak, or sometimes The Royal Oak. The village, and the pub, dated back hundreds of years, it was a fascinating place. Outside the pub was an old oak tree, hence the name, the story goes that when Oliver Cromwell was subduing England his soldiers cornered King Charles II in the area, the King escaped by hiding in the hollowed out bowl of this very tree. The pub itself was certainly old with low-beamed ceilings, you had to stoop to go through the doors. We used to walk over to this pub in the evenings during that summer of 1956 and enjoy a few beers, it was one aspect of the English lifestyle that I really enjoyed.

The local flying area was interesting. The Provost was not a high performance aeroplane, all our flying was done below 10,000 feet and this enabled us to have a good look at the countryside. There was Ely Canal, which showed up as a long straight line on the ground and the Cathedral. Ely Cathedral, one of England's finest, was right in our area. These two prominent ground features were useful landmarks that enabled us to determine just where we were from time to time. Two big American airbases, Lakenheath and Mildenhall, were in the area as well. These places were used by America's SAC, Strategic Air Command, they were home to a lot of B47 Bombers which were the Americans primary nuclear strike aircraft during the Cold War. The standoff between NATO and the Soviet's was intensifying during the 1950s, there was a large build up of military forces going on in Europe. These things were of little significance to us, we were a bit naïve about just what was going on in the world at that time. This was all about to change dramatically in the not too distant future and I was to become deeply involved in the Cold War.

On several occasions while flying in the Feltwell area I came across an unusual looking aircraft that looked like a large glider. It had very long narrow wings and what appeared to be a jet engine in the fuselage, nobody seemed to know what it was. It appeared to be flying out of Lakenheath, several other pilots at Feltwell had seen it as well. We were later to learn that this was a U2 reconnaissance plane. It was used for very high altitude intelligence gathering over the Soviet Union. As far as the Americans were concerned the aircraft did not exist however it was just about impossible to keep it a secret when it could be clearly seen flying around the Norfolk area. The whole U2 operation hit the headlines a few years later when the Soviet's managed to bring one down over Russia in 1960 and capture the pilot, Gary Powers. It was this incident that caused the failure of the East West Summit talks in Paris that year. It had been four years prior to that, in 1956, when we had seen the U2s over Norfolk in England so it was pretty obvious they had been operating for quite some time before their existence became public knowledge.

During our time at Feltwell we took to going down to London. There were three other New Zealand students at Feltwell on the course one ahead of ours. They were on the same contract with the RAF as us and had been in England for several months. They too had expected to go straight onto jet training after arriving from New Zealand but somewhere along the line the system had failed them as well so here they were on piston Provosts. We had arrived late, missed our jet course, so we too were on a Provost course. The end result, five Kiwis who were not very happy. One of these fellows had some Kiwi mates in London who had a flat. Well that was a bit of an irresistible temptation, off we went at the weekends and dumped ourselves upon the flat dwellers. We slept on couches and floors and always had a good time. We were introduced to London pub life and pub food, hmm, not quite mother's cooking and the beer was warm. I remember becoming rather fond of Watneys Red Barrel but phew did it get you bloated, you could not take too much of that. We also had our first encounter with English girls, certainly different to the Kiwi ones, the accents! One day we took ourselves off to a dance at the Hammersmith Town Hall, one of the flat dwellers reckoned it was just the greatest place to meet girls. Not that great we thought, or was that just sour grapes because we did not do so well there? We figured our chances were much better in the pubs. We spent some time during our visits to London having an even better look around than we had done earlier from Hendon, fascinating place London. The fellows in the flat were all school teachers, they were teaching in a secondary modern school in the local area, we went along to have a look. What a shock, school? more like a back street slum, not much learning being done, in fact the so called school appeared to be quite a dangerous place. Our teacher friends explained that the secondary modern was at the bottom of the system, teaching jobs were easy to come by, nobody wanted them. That suited the Kiwis, the money was good and they did not have a problem with the intimidating ways of the pupils. Certainly different to school in New Zealand. One of the fellows had bought a London taxi, he intended to take it back to New Zealand where he was convinced he would make a bit of money on it. He was planning on driving it most of the way, interesting, I never did hear how his grand plan worked out. This Kiwi flat had become popular with a group of English girls who had taken to just arriving on the doorstep from time to time much to the delight of the residents. This happened once when we were there, I was impressed. Here we were up in the wilds of Norfolk on a military base, girls did not just turn up on our doorstep. Another place we frequented in London was the Gremlin Club in Craven Hill Gardens. It was in a basement in one of those long rows of residential buildings that line the streets in London, it was frequented mainly by RAF pilots with a colonial connection, great place. Bar downstairs, another upstairs and above that good accommodation at a reasonable cost. We had a lot of fun at the Gremlin Club. All sorts of characters would turn up, nearly all RAF pilots from all over the place, ex-pats predominated. Australians, South Africans,

Rhodesians, Canadians, plenty of Kiwis, and yes, some English fellows. Most of them were on operational squadrons and were in London for a couple of days for various reasons, the Gremlin Club was a 'must visit.' We were just a couple of very junior trainee pilots who could not spin a very good yarn yet and we were just a wee bit out of our comfort zone. The place was run by a jovial Irishman, Paddy of course, I'm sure he had a surname but I never knew what it was. Quite often someone would bring their girlfriend into the club, it was a good place and the company was excellent, not a good idea. The place was full of young jet jocks and a female, any female, was fair game. I got the impression the girls rather liked all the attention.

Back to Feltwell. We completed the Provost flying, top of the class of course, well we did have a huge advantage, and prepared for the move to No:8 Flying Training School at Swinderby for the advanced stage on Vampires, jets at last. We had been in the Air Force fifteen months and were only half way through our wings course, this was taking an awfully long time. Swinderby was a big RAF Station located alongside the Fosse Way, an old Roman road that connects the city of Bath, in the southwest of England, to the cathedral city of Lincoln, in the eastern part of the country, Swinderby was about halfway between Newark, a small market town, and Lincoln. No: 8 Flying Training School was located at Swinderby and specialised in training jet pilots. There were several courses running at any one time, a lot of flying activity. All the training was done in Vampire T11s a specialized two seat training aircraft, solo flying was done on Vampire 5s, retired single seat jet fighters. Finally, sixteen months after joining the Air Force with over 200 hours in my logbook, I got to fly a jet. Nine short trips with an instructor then on September 3rd 1956 I flew solo in a Vampire, I was nineteen years old. There was a lot of instruction at Swinderby, aerobatics, high level aerobatics, stalling, spinning, high speed high altitude flight, navigation exercises, and a big emphasis on instrument flying. It was at Swinderby during this early part of our jet flying that I got to go way up high for the first time in my life, 40,000 feet in a T11 with an instructor, quite an eerie experience. The idea was to demonstrate how an aircraft's performance drops

Vampire T11

away in the thin air at altitude, there is little margin for error. The instructor attempted a high altitude loop that he managed to achieve, then he invited me to do the same. Not the greatest, the T11 just did not respond as it would at lower altitude where the air is much denser, we finished up diving down pretty much out of control. Point made, things are different at altitude. As we became more proficient, formation flying was introduced then tail chasing, night flying, and some low flying. The training was intense and continued for nine months. On April 17th 1957 I received my Royal Air Force Wings at a ceremony at Swinderby, it had taken two long years. I had 325 hours in my logbook.

The wings ceremony was a rather hollow affair for Peter and myself, we did not have any family there. The English lads had proud Mums and Dads, Aunties, Cousins, whole extended families, we had no

RAF Wings – April 1957

one, they were all on the other side of the world. In the 1950s you could not just whizz over to England, there were no big jets, it was a major ocean voyage.

At Swinderby some of the fellows on our wings course acquired cars, pretty important asset a car, gave you access to a whole new social life it also made you popular with your mates. Friday nights were pub nights. We used to go to the Saracens Head a pub in the centre of Lincoln the nearest town. Cranwell, the Royal Air Force College, was just down the road near the village of Sleaford, the career lads from 'Sleaford Tech' as Cranwell was known would be

RAF Wings Course

in the Saracens as well. Plenty of rivalry between the two groups, competition for the pretty English girls was intense. There were several Iraqi students at Swinderby, we had one of them on our course. These fellows were in the Iraqi Air Force. They had been sent to England to learn to fly jets. The UK Government of the day was supplying the Iraqi Air Force with Hunter fighters and these fellows were going to fly them. They were a privileged lot with plenty of money, amongst other things, they all bought new cars. We were not envious, well not very! I became friendly with a chap called Fathlie, a tall handsome fellow who had a new Zephyr Six. I remember going to a pub in nearby Newark one evening with Fathlie, boy did he pull the girls, I sort of felt a bit like a bee buzzing around a honey pot, 'ahem' my name's Rex and I come from New

Zealand.' The Iraqis had a hard time at Swinderby, they were not naturals at flying however the politics of the day required them to graduate. This was a bit unfortunate because if the standards being applied to us were applied to them then I don't think too many of the Iraqis would have gained their wings. This was disastrous for one of them, he killed himself in a spectacular accident. The fellow had been struggling to make the grade, he should have been chopped long before however the instructors had been told to persevere. He managed to land a Vampire 5 very heavily, it bounced back into the air and came down sideways, smashed into the ground, burst into flames and cartwheeled down the runway in a flaming ball. This shook up the Iraqis and shortly after this incident one of them packed it in and went home. I think three of them eventually succeeded in getting RAF wings. I often wonder whatever became of those Iraqis.

There was a Syrian Air Force pilot on another course at Swinderby, similar circumstances to the Iraqis, he got himself into big trouble one evening, he pulled a knife during a dispute in the mess bar. He was sent home the next day. A few weeks later one of the fellows received a letter from him, posted in Moscow, he was training on MIGs with the Russians.

The scheme under which Peter and myself joined the RAF extended to other Commonwealth countries as well. There were three Rhodesians on a course just ahead of us along with a South African. It was the first time I had come across colonials from the southern part of Africa, I was intrigued by their accents. 'Hute min, these yorpies had a very strange accent indeed.' The chap from South Africa was not happy, he found himself the victim of politics. It was 1956, South Africa was pressing to become a republic something they achieved in 1961. The Royal Air Force did not employ non commonwealth citizens so if this fellow with the South African passport was to become the holder of a republican passport in the near future then the RAF would have to terminate his training now. The alternative was for him to become a British citizen. The poor fellow; this fiercely loyal South African, as all South Africans are, had to take out British citizenship if he wanted to continue in the RAF. When we met him he had just done this, he was not very happy about it.

I feel I should comment here about 'commitment.' Peter Dwyer and I had made a huge commitment to get where we were. There were two other students on our course who intended to remain in the RAF and another six fellows who were all doing their National Service. In England at that time compulsory National Service was a requirement for all young men. The vast majority of them completed two years in the military, usually in some pretty ordinary role. A lucky few who applied, who had what it takes and who survived the selection process were trained as jet pilots, achieved RAF pilot's wings, then returned to civilian life. The six National Service fellows on our course had it made, they were being presented with the world on a platter and appeared to be taking it all for granted, none of them intended to pursue a career in aviation. They were keen enough, it's just that I could not come to grips with the fact that none of them intended to take advantage of the extraordinary opportunity they were presented with to continue on in the aviation world.

Some of the flying at Swinderby, unfortunately, had fatal consequences. One of the exercises was called a tail chase, this involved four Vampires flying along one behind another, each one slightly below the one in front in order to avoid its jet wash. The lead aeroplane then starts diving all over the sky and the other three follow closely, great fun unless you were the last one, number four, tail end charlie. He had a hard time keeping up and quite often had to pull a lot of G. This was ok except that some of the older Vampire 5s were a bit too old, and a bit 'twisted.' The Vampire is a twin boom aircraft, the tail plane and elevator are fitted between the two booms aft of the fuselage. At high speed, turbulence from the fuselage can start to reduce the effectiveness of the elevator and if the aircraft is a bit 'twisted' then the aerodynamics may not be quite what the aircraft's designer intended. There were two fatal accidents at Swinderby in quick succession where the number four in a tail chase dived into the ground at very high speed. Shortly after this there was another incident where the number four in a tail chase found himself heading for the ground fast, unable to pull up. He managed to bail out and his story caused a bit of a rethink about tail chasing. Apparently he had been pulling a lot of G and had managed to flick stall the aircraft, something you can do if you pull too much G at speed. A flick stall is a condition where one wing stalls slightly before the other one, the aircraft rolls rapidly towards the stalled wing, or flicks. He finished up in a high-speed dive and the elevators were not responding so he extended the airbrakes to reduce the speed but he got the wrong lever and lowered the undercarriage instead. The next thing the aircraft was juddering all over the sky completely out of control. He managed to jettison the canopy and bail out which is not the easiest thing to do in a Vampire 5, there's no ejector seat. Lowering the undercarriage at high speed had wrecked the aircraft but it did slow it down sufficiently to allow him to bail out. This fellow was all of twenty years of age. Shortly after these incidents all the Vampire 5s at Swinderby were air tested and several found wanting, the majority of them were retired permanently. The replacements were Vampire 9s, same type of aircraft but not as old. One day a very shaken up young fellow came back from a tail chase, number four again, with a good story to tell. He had pulled a lot of G, flick stalled and spun, however when the aircraft would not respond to normal spin recovery procedure he had decided to bail out. He jettisoned the canopy and suddenly the aircraft was no longer spinning, ok, guess I will not jump out. What had happened was the aircraft had stalled and entered a spin,

However, it had managed to get itself upside down so that it was spinning while it was upside down. This is a fairly rare occurrence, something we did not train for, applying normal spin recovery procedure in an inverted spin just aggravated the situation. Recognising the problem was asking a bit much from a student so we never did them but by all accounts an inverted spin appears similar to a normal spin. In this case when the canopy was jettisoned it altered the airflow over the tail plane sufficiently to cause the aircraft to recover from the spin all by itself. Another accident at around the same time happened to one of the instructors, a New Zealand chap, he dived into the ground at high speed in a Vampire 5. He was not tail chasing at the time and he was an experienced pilot, that one was never satisfactorily explained.

One day I was flying along in a Vampire, buzzing around some very tall cumulus clouds and generally exhilarating in the sheer joy of it all when I got a hell of a fright. I was doing a steep turn, pulling lots of G, around this big cloud when I met another Vampire doing the same thing coming the other way. I quickly rolled out of the turn and he must have tightened up on his turn because I saw him flick and spin. I pulled down and followed, it was a Sleaford Tech aircraft, it was still spinning when it disappeared into cloud, s—t, this could be real bad. What to do? what can I do? I flew back to Swinderby, landed and just sort of hid in a corner listening to every bit of scuttlebutt I could. Had there been an accident at Cranwell? Should I say something? After a day or so nothing came up so I guessed I was off the hook. Boy did I get a fright! Another incident happened to me at Swinderby, which, with hindsight, must have been rather amusing for those who observed it from the ground. I was doing an instrument flying exercise under the hood in a T11 with this hard-nosed instructor watching my every move when a very bright fire warning light came on. Now a fire in a jet is not something you take lightly, it can be seriously life threatening. The

Vampire's Goblin engine had a known weakness in the engine's main rotor rear bearing, it was known to fail and cause an engine fire which could quickly spread. It appeared that this is what had happened. The T11 was a later model aircraft than the 5s and 9s, it was fitted with two ejector seats so baling out was greatly simplified and could be achieved at relatively short notice however it could not be done at too low an altitude. Ok, Mr Instructor, instruct me, I don't think this is part of what we are supposed to be doing. The instructor was just as shaken as I was. 'Right, let's get this thing back to Swinderby, it's a T11, we don't want to lose it.' We headed for home, how bad is the fire, does it warrant jumping out, no, then let's get it back on the ground. We are trailing smoke, we're definitely on fire, I think we have a chance. We managed it, landed and got the full fire services treatment. As we rolled to a stop the instructor simply said, 'get out of here!' The story was related to us by our buddies on the ground about how this aeroplane, trailing lots of smoke, had barely stopped on the runway when the canopy opened, two bodies leapt out and took off in opposite directions, well one took off the other did a back flip on the wing. That was me, the intercom cord from my helmet was still attached to the bang seat.

Our Flight Commander at Swinderby was a Major Benevent, an American Air Force Officer on an exchange posting, we did not get on very well with the good Major. Peter and I, being colonials, were always pushing the limits a bit, something the British seemed to understand, I think it was something they liked to see. Major Benevent, on the other hand, was not very understanding. I think the Major was a little uncomfortable amongst all these British people. We got right offside with him at Christmastime 1956. We went down to London and spent Christmas with the guys in the flat, we had a memorable time, maybe a bit too memorable, we were a day late getting back to Swinderby. The Major gave us a severe telling off and threatened to terminate our training. 'Whoops Peter I think we're in trouble here.' We very quickly changed our ways, particularly when the Major was around.

Towards the end of my time at Swinderby I came into possession of a car, a very old car, the original Morris 8, well it could have been it was so old, but it was a car and a car made a big difference to your life. We also met another New Zealand chap who was at Cranwell, he was cleaning up all the honours on his course there. He invited Peter and myself to his graduation, he wanted some 'family' around when he collected all the silverware. Well did we get into trouble. We took a couple of girls from Lincoln along, we had a car and with a car you can do these things. It was a great night, Cranwell sure knew how to lay it on however it was around nine the next morning when we got these girls home. The scene was like something out of a movie. Dad was waiting on the doorstep, we were lucky to survive his wrath. I did manage to see that girl again, I was rather fond of her, but don't ever let Dad find out!

Not long before we received our Wings there was a radical shake up in the RAF, it brought about a dramatic change in my career prospects, in fact it changed the whole direction of my life. A politician called Duncan Sandys, the UK's Secretary of State for Defence, announced that fighter aircraft were now obsolete, all defence was to be done with missiles. The RAF will disband all its Venom fighter squadrons and many of the Hunter squadrons. At the time the RAF had a number of Venom squadrons in Germany and the Middle East and some Hunter squadrons in Germany and England. The disbandment occurred very quickly. Suddenly there was a glut of unemployed pilots, they were everywhere. This was disastrous, we were destined for Hunter and Venom front line squadrons. We received our wings and waited nervously for postings. Normally we could expect to go to Chivenor for Hunter conversion or Pembrey for Venoms. Then we hear that Pembrey is to close, things were looking bleak. Then a posting, one of the brand new pilots from our course is posted to RAF 'Nowhere' as the Assistant Equipment Officer, what's going on? Suddenly there are no flying jobs. Then another posting, Assistant Station Adjutant, it's getting worse. I was called in and asked if I would accept a flying job as a co-pilot on Hastings transport aircraft, 'ah, well not really, I have come all the way from New Zealand to fly jets sir.' 'Ah, well Pilot Officer Mangin, that's not going to happen, I strongly advise you to take up this offer.' 'Ah, well, if you say so sir.' 'Good, I think you have made a wise choice.' Yeah, right! This turn of events changed the whole course of my life. It turned out that this offer had a silver lining, I did not quite see it that way at the time. As I had indicated my agreement I was posted to RAF Dishforth for a short conversion course onto Hastings aircraft right away. Two days later I moved to Dishforth in Yorkshire. I said my farewells to Peter Dwyer, we had been together for two eventful years, it was unlikely we would ever be together again. Peter remained at Swinderby for several weeks and got lucky, he secured a rare posting to Chivenor to convert onto Hunters. Unfortunately for him his luck ran out at Chivenor, he flunked the course, me, well off to Dishforth. I drove the Morris 8 up to Yorkshire, it only just made it and I set about trying to sell it, I think I gave it away in the end. Carless again and my flying career did not look promising. Short course was right, just ten days. 'Read all this bumph,' three trips in a Hastings, two during the day, one at night, don't touch anything unless you are asked, now you are a qualified Hastings co-pilot. Again, I did not quite see it that way. After two years of intensive training I was being fobbed off as a co-pilot doing virtually nothing. One bright note, there was a Chipmunk at Dishforth. I talked the local instructor into checking me out. A Chipmunk was another very successful aeroplane made by

The de Havilland Aircraft Company, the same people who made the Tiger Moth. A small all metal two seat monoplane widely used for pilot training, fully aerobatic so I vented my frustration doing aerobatics.

Hastings Captains were drawn from experienced pilots who had completed a couple of operational tours, they spent eight months at Dishforth and really learnt the ropes, climatology around the world, serious navigation and a lot of flying. The Hastings was not an easy aeroplane to fly and they would be flying it to the far corners of the earth. I was not quite sure what I was expected to do, I did not consider myself qualified to do much at all on a Hastings, perhaps it might be different on a squadron. 'You come from New Zealand right?' 'Yep.' 'Well in that case you will be on 24 Commonwealth Squadron.' This was where my luck turned, the following two years were to take me around the world, expose me to nuclear testing in the Pacific, take me all over Africa, the Middle East, outback Australia, and pop me down on Waikiki Beach with lots of money in my pocket. Flying in the Pacific made a huge impression on me and caused me to think seriously about the future. It was while I was on 24 Squadron I made the decision to leave the RAF at the eight-year point in my contract, return to New Zealand and fly for TEAL, New Zealand's international airline. All these things happened.

Eventually I spent thirty years flying big jets around the Pacific and the World, however back to 1957, I was off to No: 24 Commonwealth Squadron at RAF Colerne, near Bath.

No: 24 Commonwealth Squadron

I arrived in Bath on the train, a beautiful old Roman town and caught a bus to Colerne. My worldly possessions, two suitcases, accompanied me. Down to the basics now, bit awkward carting a lot of stuff around on British Rail the RAF's preferred method of travel. Colerne was on a hilltop quite close to Bath in the southwest of England. An old pre-war RAF station with big solid brick buildings. The Officers Mess was a comfortable 1930s style double storey building, a delightful spot. I moved into a large room, all my own, spread my few possessions around, then made my way across the airfield to 24 Squadron and introduced myself. The CO was an Australian Air Force Wing Commander on an exchange posting. The Squadron included several exchange crews from Commonwealth countries and some RAF crews. Three Australian, one New Zealand, one Canadian, and about eight RAF crews. The RAF element was full of ex-pats like myself, it really was a Commonwealth Squadron, perhaps this might be ok after all.

24 was currently flying all the transport support for Operation Grapple, the British nuclear testing programme being conducted at Christmas Island, just south of Hawaii in the Pacific. Crews were being deployed to Christmas Island for two and three-month detachments on an ongoing basis with around four crews and aircraft on the island at any one time, this sounded pretty interesting. In no time at all I was scheduled to go off on one of these detachments. Things were looking up, hang on, shouldn't I perhaps become a bit more proficient on the Hasting aircraft first. Right now I know precious little about the aircraft or this transport flying business. I do know how to fly a jet though, anybody listening? 'You will learn laddie, on the job training.'

My very first flying job on 24 Squadron was to assist in flying a Hastings to Swinderby, picking up a load of paratroops, and dropping them over Cranwell. The Hastings Captain was a very experienced fellow, just as well because I knew nothing about anything. I could help him out with Swinderby though, I had just left the place. The sight of all those Vampires roaring around was a bit hard to take and when I met some fellow students who I knew who were still there, they were a bit agog about my change of fortune. Dropping army paratroops was a major role for 24 Squadron, I was involved with it frequently during those first few weeks on the squadron, then just eight weeks after I had gained my RAF, wings I was off around the world to Christmas Island.

The Hastings was the backbone of Transport Command in the 1950s. A big heavy four engined piston aircraft designed to carry freight but it did not have a very long range, there were some places in the world that it could not get to. One of the routes that was just a bit too long for a Hastings was California to Hawaii. This meant that to get to Christmas Island in the Pacific we could not go the short way across America, we had to go the long way through the Middle East, Far East, Australia, then up through the Pacific, all this sounded pretty exciting stuff. We set off for Christmas Island in July 1957. There were six of us in the crew. The Captain, 28 years old, very experienced, he knew all about Hastings. The Co-pilot, me, all of 20 years old, I knew precious little about what we were about to do. Then there was a Navigator, a Flight Engineer, a Signaller, and a Quartermaster. These fellows were all hoary old NCOs, Non Commissioned Officers, who had seen service in the Second World War, they were old enough to be my father. Being the youngest officer in the crew meant that I landed the job of looking after the money, the dreaded imprest account. It was a large steel box with a big lock and key and it was full of money and promissory notes. A promissory note was a document that could be presented to financial institutions around the world stating that the British Government would honour the note up to the value detailed on it and some of these values were big, like £10,000. As the imprest account holder I had to pay the bills and the crew for the next two and a half months. This box of cash became the bane of my life, I finished up sleeping with the damn thing on occasions. Wherever we finished up each day I would have to seek out a secure place to stash the imprest. The old hands on the crew eyed this box of money with covetous eyes and during the course of the next couple of months I was to learn the many and devious ways of creative accounting. From England our route to Christmas Island took us south to Idris, then El Adam, both old Italian airfields in Libya. Idris was a joint civilian and military field about twenty miles inland from Tripoli, Libya's capital city, it was not a particularly impressive sight, a few scrawny camels wandering around a sandy field with a strip of tarseal on it, a few date palms, plenty of flies, sweltering hot. El Adam, which is not far from Tobruk, of World War II fame, was not much better, hot, sandy and little else. On to Habbaniya near Baghdad in Iraq, again not very impressive, more sand, heat, and flies. Then Karachi located on the coast in Pakistan, it was different, a big middle eastern city, something I had not experienced before. From there we flew to Negombo in Ceylon, Changi in Singapore, Labuan in Borneo, Darwin and Amberley in Australia, then out into the Pacific; Nandi in Fiji, Canton Island, and finally to Christmas Island itself. It took us eleven days, we flew all day every day, a total of 78 flying hours. Our cargo consisted of 70 British soldiers who were all destined to be cannon fodder for the nuclear testing at Christmas. All this was effectively in the hands of one 28 year old pilot, I was not qualified to actually fly the aeroplane, in fact I was not qualified to do very much at all. That's the way it was in the 1950s. Once we got to Christmas we were employed on supply runs to Honolulu in the north and Australia to the south, we did a lot of flying and I just loved every minute of it.

There were a few occurrences during that trip that I must tell you about. Karachi, not the greatest of places. We landed at the civilian airport there late one afternoon and were taken to Minwalla's Guest House located at Ismalia, a Karachi suburb, what a dump! We had a few beers, a meal and that was it, off to bed, there was no time to socialise, our flying schedule was pretty savage, we were tired. The next morning, crook, the trots, bad, must have been the food. During the following two years I passed through Karachi several times, every time the same thing, the trots. On the last occasion that I transited the place nothing passed my lips, no food, no drink, I did not even clean my teeth, I still got the trots, must be in the air. On this first occasion we got out to the airport in the morning to fly off to our next exotic port of call, Negombo in Ceylon, the need to go was very strong. I must have checked every toilet in the airport terminal, I could not believe what I found, they were not just dirty, they were unbelievably filthy, all overflowing with excrement, it was all over the floors as well, no way could I go. I remember having to eventually use the port-a-loo in the aircraft, which was not the greatest, the temperature in there must have been up in the 50s, it was so hot I was almost passing out. This experience scarred me for life. Ever since that day I've had this recurring dream about having to go and not being able to find a decent toilet. The whole crew had the same problem, the trip to Negombo became a real endurance test. The troops we were carrying were just as bad. They had been accommodated at a military barracks in Karachi and sure enough, the trots. At Negombo, which is just up the coast from the capital, Colombo in Ceylon, now called Sri Lanka, we went body surfing. We had got over our ailment and the crashing surf at the local beach was just what we needed. I had a haircut and neck massage at a local barbers shop, I have never experienced anything like it since, boy did that massage make me feel good. While I was being sent to dreamland the barber was trying very hard to sell me a ruby, they were common in Ceylon, the price was right as well. He should have known that RAF Officers are always broke. I very much fitted that mould and I knew absolutely nothing about rubies. An interesting snippet, apparently Ceylon at that time had the highest murder rate in the world, 'really, I had better watch my back.' 'Don't worry they only murder each other, never foreigners.'

We continued on to Changi in Singapore arriving late one afternoon and were accommodated in the RAF Officers Mess, which was quite close to Changi village. This was the first time I had been in the Far East, a whole new experience. We enjoyed a fascinating evening in the village. I had my very first authentic Chinese meal and sampled some Tiger beer, another first. I was soon to learn that all the Asian countries make excellent beer, and the shops, everything was for sale, just everything.

The idea was to fly to Darwin the next morning however the direct flight was just beyond the range of a Hastings so a refuelling stop at Labuan would be required. Labuan is a small island off the coast of Sabah in North Borneo. Our departure from Changi was delayed for some reason and we finished up being late, we had to spend a night at a local hotel in Labuan. When we went out to the airfield the following morning something did not look right with our plane, it had sunk into the hardstand. A Hastings has one very large wheel on each of the two undercarriage legs, these two big wheels impose quite a high load on the tarmac. I think the aircraft must have been parked overnight on a part of the tarmac that was not quite up to scratch, whatever the reason it appeared that the loading imposed by the wheels had exceeded the strength of the tarmac, they had sunk right in. We had damaged the tarmac and were stuck, what to do? Our hard working Captain, assisted by me of course, organised the local engineering services to come up with some large jacks and related gear and the problem was resolved. Labuan was a civilian airfield, I think the RAF might have received a bill for the damage to their tarmac. While all this was going on I struck up a conversation with a couple of Cathay pilots. These fellows were Australians, they had a C46 transport plane at Labuan. The C46 was an oversize DC3 built by the Curtis company in America. Cathay, a new Hong Kong based airline, had several of them. These fellows suggested that I might like to come and work for them, they were actively looking for pilots and a keen young New Zealander, RAF trained, was just the sort of fellow they wanted. 'I'm actually jet trained' I offered, just thought I would throw that in. 'Well that's even better, when can you start.' 'Ahh! well! I'm sort of tied up here for a few years however I will keep it in mind, and thanks for the offer.' I've often thought about 'what might have been' had I taken them up on that offer. We flew out of Labuan for the long trip to Darwin and arrived late. It was the first time I had set foot in Australia, I liked it from day one, and the Australians? they were good guys, just don't tell them. We spent the night at the Australian Air Force base in Darwin, it was pretty comfortable except for the toilets, what toilets again? Well the toilets were ok, it was the livestock that inhabited them. There I was sitting on the throne doing my thing when splat, something cold and slimy attached itself to my bottom, yuk! I leapt off the toilet and a large toad flopped onto the floor. 'What the:' apparently the local toads like to live around the bend in the toilet, when there's a bit of activity they come out to play. The fix, flush the toilet before being seated that gives you a bit of time but no one told us that. On the next visit to the toilet I investigated, I lifted the top of the cistern, there were these eyes looking back at me, the toads were in there as well, different!

Next day we flew south across Australia, another first, what an incredible experience, the place is so big. Being brought up in New

Zealand I found it difficult to comprehend the vast distances in Australia, everything is so far away from everything else. Our Hastings flew at a relatively low height, it was not very fast either, it took hours and hours to fly across the vastness that was the Australian outback, there was plenty of time to take it all in. The country below was a monotonous brown with little variation, it appeared to be very arid. There were patches of green here and there, a small creek or a water hole. Occasionally a road or a fence would appear as a long straight line and break the monotony of it all, it was just so vast. There was the occasional settlement, small areas of human habitation set in this arid wasteland that stretched to the horizon in all directions. This first experience took us across Queensland in the north east of the country flying from Darwin to Brisbane. On some later trips to Australia I would get to fly over the central part of the country, that was even more impressive, virtually all desert, vast dried up lakebeds. Very occasionally a small plume of dust could be seen on one of the few straight lines on the surface, a motor vehicle, way out in the middle of nowhere, there was life down there.

We arrived at Amberley, a big RAAF base near Brisbane, in the afternoon, there was still a bit of daytime left so we went into the local town, Ipswich, what an experience. The outback, as Hollywood would have you believe, except it was real. It was a Saturday, the whole place was jumping, a pub on every corner, bat wing doors swinging wildly, drinkers falling in and out, it was the wild west, is this what Australia is really like? A first experience I will never forget, but it was Queensland, they are different in Queensland, just ask any Australian. We had a 'middy' or two and some 'schooners,' I just love those Australian expressions, we got back to Amberley rather late, what an introduction. The following morning it was out across the Pacific to Fiji and up to Canton Island. Canton existed to service Pan American's Clippers which operated between Australia and the US. They were big four engined Boeing Stratoliners, they did not have the range to fly very long legs, hence the requirement for a refuelling stop at Canton. This was pretty handy because we had a range problem as well and needed to refuel when flying between Fiji and Christmas. We arrived at Canton Island one warm afternoon, it looked like a slice of heaven to me, I had not seen a real beach since leaving New Zealand more than two years before, I rushed into the sea and revelled in it all. The whole place was a mini America run by Pan Am, a big open-air cinema, a mess hall where cookie did over easy eggs, what's an over easy egg? I was initiated there and then and I've had a love affair with them ever since. After a pleasant night on Canton we departed in the morning for the final leg to Christmas.

Flying over the Pacific had its moments. The Hastings was not a sophisticated aircraft and one of its shortcomings was weather radar, there wasn't any. This became a problem because in the Pacific you get extensive areas of thunderstorm activity that it's advisable to avoid. This is just about impossible when you are flying in cloud and cannot see the towering thunderstorm clouds, that's what weather radar's for. We did have a couple of ADFs, automatic direction finders and these could be utilised as thunderstorm detectors. An ADF can be tuned to a specific radio frequency, it will then point, with a needle on an instrument, at any transmission source on that frequency. This allows the use of various radio stations as navigation aids, it's a good system widely used in aviation. A lightning bolt in a thunderstorm transmits on a broad spectrum of frequencies and an ADF needle will invariably be deflected towards a lightening flash, 'a thunderstorm detector.' So here you are crashing along in cloud, icing up, getting thrashed by the turbulence and all the time you have to make sure that you catch the ADF during the next lightning flash and make sure the needle does not point dead ahead, that was the theory, bit hard in practice. We really did have to avoid these storms, they were dangerous. The Hastings was a very strong aircraft, just as well because some of the turbulence we flew through over the Pacific really tested the structural limits of that aircraft. Most of our flying was done around 10,000 feet, about the worst possible altitude to fly through a thunderstorm.

Flying over the Pacific Ocean was another whole new experience, the distances involved were huge, it took hours and hours just to get from one place to the next. It takes a while to comprehend the vastness of this ocean, I found the whole experience quite extraordinary.

Christmas Island was an interesting place, 100 miles north of the equator and 1200 miles south of Honolulu; it's one of the more remote atolls in the Line Islands, now called Kiribati. A standard coral atoll, similar to the ones found all over the Pacific. Christmas was big, one of the biggest in the world. It's covered in coconut palms all growing in straight lines, hang on, nature does not have straight lines. The story goes that in the late 1800s Lever's Pacific Plantations, an America company, had moved in and established a copra plantation. They planted thousands of coconut palms, hence the straight lines. The operation had been abandoned a few years later and all these trees have been growing and producing coconuts ever since. All the rotting fruit on the ground has given rise to a huge population of land crabs that feed on it. When we were on the island the crab population was estimated at about 120 million, yes that's right, 120 million. The food supply was huge, so were the crabs, both in size and numbers, they measured anything up to twenty plus centimetres across, they were everywhere. There were several different species but one in particular seemed to dominate, a large fellow called Cardisomia Carnifex. I should mention here that there are two Christmas Islands, the other one is an Australian possession in the Indian Ocean, it too has land crabs, in fact the whole of the Indian Ocean, all the islands to the north of Australia and the whole of the Pacific, have land crabs. They are all of similar varieties and are very common.

Christmas had two small settlements, London and Paris, one on either side of the main entrance to the lagoon. A road connected London, on the north side, to the main base camp then continued on to the airfield. It was formed from crushed coral and had become surfaced with crab shell. The crabs liked to sit on this road but they were no match for the big low pressure tyres of the Landrovers that used it, it was a busy road. When a crab was run over it made a pop sound and some more shell was added to the road surface. It had become a bit of one-upmanship to see how many 'pops' you could score driving between the camp and the airfield. The road was a hazardous place, not just for crabs, there were these Landrovers swerving all over the place trying to score pops.

Crabs were inescapable, they were everywhere, it was not possible to ignore them, they became part of our lives. Harmless enough, frightening appearance but harmless, not so sure about that big claw, looked pretty powerful to me, I never tried to find out either. We played games with them, the things they appeared to be able to do, drink beer, play the beat up mess piano, write with a pencil held in a claw, eat at the table, they became our buddies. Then there were some things we did that were definitely not crab friendly, like crab golf. This was a late night activity that required the participant to be somewhat intoxicated and living on a coral atoll, that was just about every night. We slept in tents on low camp beds that were sitting directly on the coral, no flooring, these tents were located just above a beach. At bedtime, and that could be pretty late, the idea was to walk along the beach to your tent. The coral at the top of the beach formed a small ledge or overhang, the crabs liked to sit along this ledge, bit like a line of golf balls on golf tees, we would get a piece of driftwood and try out our golfing prowess using the crabs for golf balls, not very nice when you think about it, the golf balls never went very far, they tended to disintegrate. Oh yes, sleeping in those tents, time for the crabs revenge. There you were snoring away on this very low camp bed with the blankets draped over the coral on either side, you would be awakened by this noise, the crabs made a bit of a racket moving over the coral, the noise would get closer, it was a crab on a mission, your bed was in its path. No problem, the crab just went up over and down the other side, terrifying when it first happened, but just old hat after a while, then there was the fishing. Apparently the powers that be required a

Hastings At Christmas

certain weight of fish to be taken from local waters and be tested for radioactivity. This was to prove that what the British were doing at Christmas Island was not dangerous and thus appease public opinion, yeah right! Well there were two ways of doing this, catch a lot of small fish, or catch a few big fish, the big fish option caught our attention. What we required was a big hook, big bait, big heavy line and we needed to get out into deep water. There was a Sikorsky helicopter at Christmas that was used for search and rescue purposes, we put the hard word on the pilot and bingo, some of the world's very first heli fishing. The technique we devised was to use a long piece of chain, a huge hook, and whatever piece of carcase we could con from the mess kitchen. We would fly the chopper out beyond the main reef and lower the carcass into the water on the big hook at the end of the chain. Well some of the results were spectacular. On one occasion a huge shark chomped the carcase, could not chomp through the chain, and was hooked. Now what? The shark's thrashing about on the end of the chain was causing problems for the chopper pilot, suddenly our novel heli fishing became a bit risky. We dragged the shark through a gap in the reef, across the lagoon and up onto the beach where we dropped the chain. 'There you are, fish!'

Soon after I arrived on the island there was a rather sad incident. One of the young conscripts who had travelled out with us on our Hastings was killed. This young chap had never been outside England in his short life and suddenly he found himself on a tropical South Sea Island with all this sun, sand and surf. It was all a bit much, he was way outside his comfort zone, could not comprehend it all. He waded out across the lagoon and dived into the breaking surf on the main reef. Well the surf just picked him up and dumped him back onto the coral, the very jagged coral When they got him onto the operating table in the hospital there was not much that could be done, he had been torn to pieces by the coral and died.

The Officers Mess on the island was home for an old beat up piano that a few of the fellows could play. Invariably, late at night, everybody would be subjected to someone's fantastic piano playing. The poor piano had beer spilt over it, constantly, lots of beer at times, it had a terrible life then one night it was murdered. After a particularly hard drinking session it was decided the piano did not sound that good anymore, must be getting old, deserves a respectable burial. The piano was carted down to the lagoon and thrown in. The next morning, whoops, what did we do to the piano? I think we might have damaged it. Down to the lagoon, too late, far too late, the long serving piano was a heap of matchwood in the lagoon. Oops, how do we explain this away?

From Christmas we operated a supply shuttle to Hawaii where we used the facilities at Hickam Air Force Base. Hickam was a huge American Air Force facility on the edge of Pearl Harbour alongside Honolulu International Airport, the same airport runway was used by both military and civilian aircraft. Hickam was home to what seemed like hundreds of big military transport aircraft, Douglas C124s, Globemasters, Boeing C-97 Stratocruisers, the list was endless. At that time America had a large military presence in the Far East and Japan, all this activity was in support of that presence. Everything seemed to be on a very big scale, I was impressed. Also impressive were the facilities available to us at Hickam. We stayed in the BOQs, Bachelor Officers Quarters, and we were able to use the Officers Club. This club was extraordinary, big with excellent restaurants and bars and it seemed to be full of females, good-looking females. The American Far East support operation was based at Hickam and there was a lot of through traffic from the States as well. All these females were the wives and sweethearts of all the guys who were away in the Far East, they all appeared to be out for a good time, apparently the club was a happy hunting ground. Well now, that's very interesting! Unfortunately most of our trips to Honolulu were up one day, back the next, we did not get to spend time there. One of our crew had a friend in Honolulu, a local resident. During one of our visits this chap organised a night out in Waikiki, he picked us up in his car, the biggest and shiniest thing I had ever seen and drove us in to Waikiki for a meal at a nightspot. The place was right by Diamond Head, Bobby McGee's, we had a great time. I think Bobby McGee's is still there to this day. Later that evening when we were driving back to Hickam we were involved in a minor accident, I can't remember the details, I had had a few. I do remember our host being concerned because we had some opened cans of beer in the car, in America that's a no no. We got back to Hickam ok, so I guess he must have squared things away.

On another occasion we got lucky and had a couple of days off in Honolulu. I took advantage of this and moved into the BOQs at Fort DeRussy right on Waikiki Beach. DeRussey was a military recreation establishment with superb facilities, there was a downside however, unlike the BOQs at Hickam, which were free, there was a charge for staying at DeRussy, $1 per night, yep, I can manage that, and a lot more as well, I have the imprest. Our basic pay was not that good but because we were so far away from home we were entitled to all sorts of allowances. I had the dreaded imprest so there was little trouble about the actual payment of these allowances, I was the officer responsible for paying everybody, including myself. We worked out that we were entitled to overseas allowance, operational flying allowance, foreign area allowance, hardship allowance, and some more that I cannot recall, oh yes, there was the creative accounting bit as well. All up, I had quite a bit of money in my pocket. There would be a day of reckoning however, when I got back to Colerne in England I would have to account for all this expenditure to the Station Accounts Officer. The throughput of the imprest account was huge, many thousands of pounds. The eventual day of reckoning would be interesting. I remember sitting at the excellent bar in DeRussy one evening drinking the cheaply priced beer which was available to military personnel when I struck up a conversation with an American Air Force Major, that's about equivalent to a Squadron Leader in the RAF. I was a Pilot Officer, bottom of the heap, but then I was only twenty years old. The conversation got around to money, he was rather curious about how I was finding the cost of everything here in Hawaii. He was stationed at Hickam and for him it was considered a home posting, no overseas allowances. He found the place rather expensive, his pay did not go very far. We got down to detail and it turned out that what I was paying myself from the imprest, I did not tell him that though, was about twice what he was getting. This shook him, goddam, you limies sure are well paid. I did enjoy my short stay in Waikiki, Honolulu and Hickam made a big impression.

I must tell you another story about an imprest account. One of our crews spent some time in America carrying out flying tasks related to Operation Grapple. All the expenditure was in US dollars so the young fellow running the imprest decided to cash a rather large promissory note to get some US dollars. They were operating out of McCarran Field at Las Vegas. This chap decided to do it with a touch of class. He took himself off to The Golden Nugget Casino on the Strip in Las Vegas and received the real VIP treatment. He cashed a promissory note for £5,000. This was in 1957 and that was a lot of money. The Casino presented him with a plaque stating that he was a valued customer and gave him an escort back to the airfield. Not sure what higher authority would have thought about that, it was assumed that these promissory notes would be cashed at military establishments or banks.

On another occasion while flying from Honolulu to Christmas one of our four engines failed. We were closer to Christmas than Honolulu so unfortunately we had to continue on to Christmas, pity, it could have been good for several days in Honolulu had we been closer. Engine failures were quite common on Hastings, in fact the aircraft had a reputation for being the best three engined aircraft in the RAF. The major problem was the oil cooling system, it suffered from an overheating problem called 'coring.' During my stint on

Hastings this happened on five occasions. This particular failure gave us several free days at Christmas so we enjoyed ourselves swimming and sunbathing on our tropical island, glorious but the facilities were a bit rough!

Grapple X

The nuclear testing at Christmas Island was actually conducted at a small atoll just to the south of Christmas, Malden Island. The few people who inhabited Malden were evacuated to Fanning Island away to the north as were all the native women and children who inhabited Christmas. The 2000 or so military people on Christmas remained there for the tests. This has been the subject of much controversy ever since, they did not escape unscathed. Three nuclear devices were dropped from Valiant bombers over Malden. Later in the testing programme two more powerful devices, H-bombs, were detonated over the southeast corner of Christmas Island itself. One of these tests, Grapple X, as it was known, on the 8th November 1957, did not go quite as planned. The nuclear device detonated with a much larger blast than intended, 1.8 megatons, it was meant to be 1 megaton. Considerable damage was done to the main camp on the island, some buildings were destroyed and a lot of tents knocked over. Fortunately we had left the island shortly before this incident. It was the politics of the day that brought about this dangerous situation. A partial test ban treaty was about to be agreed to by the nuclear powers that would restrict large scale atmospheric testing. Britain had not successfully tested a hydrogen bomb at this stage and it appeared they could miss the boat. To speed things up testing was moved from Malden to Christmas Island itself. This decision placed all those people on Christmas at risk, something that has had consequences in later years. Canberra aircraft were utilised as 'sniffers' immediately after these nuclear blasts, they flew through the mushroom cloud produced by the bomb and collected air samples. The pilots who flew these aircraft were exposed to considerable amounts of radiation and rumour has it that they have suffered considerably in later life. Several naval vessels were located in the testing area in an observer role and some of them were contaminated by radioactive fallout. Again, this has become a controversial matter over the years as the health of some of the people who were on those ships has deteriorated. With that wonderful thing hindsight, it has become apparent that the considerable risks taken with people's lives during operation Grapple have had unfortunate consequences. In recent years, long after these events took place, information has surfaced relating to two Royal New Zealand Navy vessels, the frigates Pukaki and Rotoiti. These two ships were deployed as weather observers. They had a combined compliment of 551 men on board and were in the testing zone for many months carrying out surveillance duties and reporting weather. Virtually all the personnel on these two ships have encountered medical problems in later years, all radiation related. The problems have arisen not from being exposed to the actual bomb blasts but by having been so long in the area. Water was limited and much use was made of rainwater for washing and drinking. It appears that the vast amounts of radiation released into the atmosphere by the tests had caused the rain over a very wide area to become mildly radioactive. In the prevailing tropical conditions very little clothing was worn and unprotected bodies were frequently exposed to rain. Prolonged exposure to rain and the drinking of rainwater caused a build up of radiation in the body that has had adverse affects in later life. When I heard about this it gave me a bit of a fright, this could be me. With hindsight however I think I may have escaped this rather grim fate. At Christmas Island I was not in the habit of standing about in the rain with very little clothing on but then I was not on a very hot metal ship either. The drinking water, well I don't think I drank any water, a lot of beer yes, but no water. As I recall the drinking water supply at Christmas was indeed rainwater. Showering; that would have been rainwater and we did take showers. Cups of tea? Well fortunately I am not a tea drinker. Actually I did not spend that much time on the island so my exposure would have been minimal. I have heard about what subsequently happened to some of the navy people who were at Christmas and I often wonder about how some of the other people who spent long periods on the island have fared.

Around the middle of September 1957 we headed off down through the Pacific to Australia on the first part of the long trip back to England. Our sojourn on Christmas had been an extraordinary experience, something I still recall vividly. Unbeknown to me at the time there would be a repeat of it all the following year. First stop Canton, refuel, then on to Nandi in Fiji, a very long day, it was about to get a whole lot longer, it was my 21st birthday. We retired to the Airport Club at Nandi for a few drinks. After a couple of months on Christmas Island there was no such thing as a few drinks most sessions resulted in drinking to excess. My good reliable mates filled me in well and truly, I think they must have sewn themselves up as well because I was not very well looked after. I recall coming to and all that was visible was this long narrow strip of sky, umm! odd! where am I? At the bottom of a monsoon ditch, the strip of sky was the view from the bottom. I had spent what was left of the night in this ditch, thanks guys. Breakfast, hmm! my mates were not looking too good either, we think we had an enjoyable night but were not too sure. It was going to be a hard day, we had to fly to Amberley near Brisbane. We survived the day, had an early night at Amberley, then on to RAAF Edinburgh, near Adelaide. Here we were to pick up some freight for transport to the UK. Amongst the 'freight' was a young Australian girl. She was a science graduate off to England to take up a post with the UK Atomic Energy Commission. The RAF had granted her officer status plus a free trip to England in a Hastings, interesting! This trip was going to take nine days, someone was going to have to keep an eye on this young lady and I am volunteering! Suddenly, being the only young fellow on the crew was a huge advantage. We had an enjoyable time, stops at Darwin and Labuan, then Changi where we went into Singapore and had a night on the town, then off to Negombo in Ceylon where we enjoyed a day off. I can't recall why we had the day off, however, I do recall vividly the day we spent together on the local surf beach body surfing. Karachi, some camel riding and unfortunately the trots again, apparently unavoidable, but not too severe this time. From

Karachi it was onto Habbaniya in Iraq. We took a taxi into Baghdad and had a quick look around, not much time to really do anything. . The taxi trip was unreal, clouds of dust prevented a clear view of the road, apparently the driver just followed the tops of the power poles that were visible above all the dust, what about the fellow coming the other way? Habbaniya was a dual civilian Iraqi Air Force field and in the Officers Mess was an Arab trader whose name was Jesus Christ, yep, true, Jesus Christ. We purchased a couple of curved daggers in beautifully engraved scabbards. I paid with an English Lloyds Bank cheque that he was quite happy to accept. This cheque duly showed up on my bank statement debited to Jesus Christ, different! I made inquiries about an Iraqi Air Force pilot named Fathlie but drew a blank. Next, El Adam, Idris, and finally England. We landed at Lyneham and spent a night in the Officers Mess there. It was a bit of a weepy affair, we had enjoyed each other's company enormously over the past nine days, now it was all over. We promised to meet again but it never happened, our lifestyles were worlds apart. The next day she went off to London, we flew on to Colerne. I had been on 24 Squadron just four months, it seemed like a lifetime. I had been around the world, well almost, and enjoyed some incredible experiences. Perhaps this posting does have a silver lining. Oh yes, I had made up my mind about just what I wanted to do with the rest of my life. One final thing, that imprest. When we arrived back at Colerne I took a day off then braced myself for a meeting with the station Accounts Officer. I had no training in accountancy this imprest thing had just been dropped on me. I had records, lots of scraps of paper on which everything, I think, was recorded. When I got to go through it all even I got lost. Well the Accounts Officer was a practical type, he had already had to deal with a lot of these imprests that had been operated by a few very junior officers, he was obviously aware that it would be virtually impossible to do a proper reconciliation. 24 Sqdn had been operating these Grapple detachments for a while, he obviously had a fair idea of just how much money would have been spent by an average crew, one hell of a lot! A few questions were asked, and it was finished, phew!

The next couple of months were taken up with paratroop dropping then a trip around the Mediterranean to Malta and Cyprus. Cyprus was interesting. EOKA, the terrorist organisation, had become a big problem. Led by a chap called General Grivas some of the Greek population on the island were conducting a terror campaign against the British to try and force ENOSIS which was the name of a movement calling for the union of Cyprus with Greece. The main victims of this campaign seemed to be British service personnel and their families. The random shooting of British pcoplc on thc street seemed to be the main danger. We spent a night in Nicosia. When we landed we were issued with service 38 revolvers and some ammunition, 'for your own protection, and please do not go out at night.' We were accommodated at the Ledra Palace hotel on Ledra Street in the center of Nicosia, murder mile, not the safest place to be. 'Do not go out,' 'ok, we will stay in.' There must have been more than thirty service personnel in the hotel bar, all with loaded 38 revolvers stuck in their belts. We had a few then went off to bed. Perhaps I had a few too many because when I got to my room I pulled this revolver out, wonder if this thing works? Bang, bang, bang, out the window, yep, it works, and went to bed. The next morning, what did I do, oh s--t, I could be in big trouble here. I sneaked about the place trying not to be noticed, nothing was said. We went out to the airfield and handed back our weapons, please oh please, do not count the ammunition. Again nothing was said. Off we went to Luqa in Malta, still nothing. Phew! You sure do some stupid things at times!

Not long after the Cyprus episode I was involved in something, that with the value of hindsight, I now realise could have involved me in some very serious trouble. I think I was set up. I got involved in gun running. At the time, late in 1957, the French were having serious problems with the FLN terrorist organisation in Algeria. The FLN, short for National Liberation Front, was at war with France. One day the Squadron Commander called me in, 'free tonight? good, I have a job for you. You are going over to Lyneham with one of our crews to do a classified job and please keep your mouth shut.' 'yes boss.' Lyneham was a large airfield in the south of England, it was the main base for RAF Transport Command. That evening I met up with the crew, it was the New Zealand exchange crew, they were short of a co-pilot, I was it. An all New Zealand crew. Off we went to Lyneham where our aircraft was loaded with some wooden crates from a large unmarked truck. I inquired from the Captain, a fairly young chap from New Zealand, 'what's the story?' 'Not sure, and please don't ask.' Hmmm, that was red rag to a bull. 'Where are we off too?' 'Ahh, you will find out once we are airborne,' really, things are getting mysterious. We took off, 'ok, where are we going?' 'El Aouina in Tunis.' 'What are we carrying?' 'You don't need to know.' 'Look I'm getting a bit pissed off with all this, what gives?' 'Well I'm pretty pissed off as well, I have been ordered to do this by the boss, I'm not sure what it's all about, but I can guess, one more thing, we are not talking on the radios and when we fly across France we switch off the navigation lights.' 'You've got to be kidding,' just about all this flight is across France in the middle of the night, without lights? Now I was really worried. 'I need a pee,' I lied. I went down the back and had a look at what we were carrying, a lot of flat wooden boxes lashed to the floor of the aircraft with no markings. I had a close look at one then forced the lid. Inside was a Thompson sub machine gun of World War Two vintage all wrapped up in greaseproof paper, shit! I returned from my pee and said nothing. I was caught up in something that could have nasty consequences, why the all New Zealand crew? We flew on, everyone was nervous, the French were not stupid, they would not hesitate to do whatever was in their best interests. We landed at El Aouina in the middle of the night, there was a reception committee waiting. We were taken into the terminal and plied with whatever we wanted. I did not want anything however this important looking well dressed chap insisted I have a cigar with him, I did, it was a very good cigar. Who he was I do not know. Our load was rapidly offloaded and disappeared into the night. It does not take too much imagination to guess where the guns went, straight across the border into Algeria and the FLN. What game the British Government was playing I cannot imagine, why the all New Zealand crew? We took off again as soon as we could and flew to Luqa in Malta landing in the small hours. The next morning we scanned every newspaper we could find, nothing! That evening we went into the capital, Valetta, and had an entertaining time in an area of the city called The Gut, not a place you would take your mother. The following day, back to the UK, still nothing in the press, in fact that was the end of it, not another word was said about the whole business. I often think, what could have been?

Later that year, 1957, I was to spend Christmas in Singapore, in hospital. I flew out along the now familiar route arriving in Changi late in December, the Karachi trots were raging, I was seriously crook. I think it might have been a bit more than just the trots because I finished up in the local military hospital and my crew abandoned me. They borrowed another co-pilot from the local Hastings Squadron at Changi and continued on to Australia. On their way back a few days later they looked in on me, flat on my back, still crook. They decided to keep their new co-pilot and set off back to England. I was a week in hospital slowly recovering then I moved into the Officer Mess at Changi, I was not pushing too hard to get back to Colerne. I took the opportunity to have a good look around Singapore and enjoyed a couple of excellent parties in the mess.

Singapore in the 1950s was a very different place to today's modern city. Orchard Road was the centre of everything as it still is and all the hotels were low rise, there were very few tall buildings. The streets were full of food stalls and the kebabs, just as good as today's, even better perhaps, it was always better in the olden days wasn't it? The Singapore River basin was a thriving place for lighters unloading cargo from the ships out in the main harbour. The area was a jungle of warehouses and old buildings, all very colourful. The shopping was great, Tiger beer was the drink of choice. Changi was a large military base used by the British, the civilian airport was at a place called Payer Lebar. There was a military airfield for combat aircraft at Tengah at the western end of the island and another at Seletar on the north side. The city streets were lined on both sides with shop-houses, buildings joined together, with a shop on the ground floor and a living area, or house, above. There was a large outdoor market called Arab Street where everything, and I mean everything, could be purchased. It took its name from the street where it was situated, Arab Street. The night time action was at a place called Bugis Street, and the 'in' eating-place was Fatties in Albert Street. There was an Indian restaurant that was used quite a bit by military people, The Banana Leaf Apollo, but it required a very strong constitution on the part of the diner, it was best described as a Café de Gutter however the food was excellent, served on large banana leaves by hand out of a big kerosene can, no eating utensils and very big bottles of Kingfisher beer. It was a bottomless meal, you could have just as much as you wanted, no extra charge, but do avoid the toilet, it was right up there with Karachi!

One attraction that made quite an impression, the Tiger Balm Gardens, a large park close to the city full of unusual and very Asian statuary, humans, animals, mythical creatures, all beautifully constructed and coloured, very lifelike. The place had been created by a wealthy Chinese family who made Tiger Balm a dark coloured ointment that was reputed to cure just about everything. Tiger Balm came in a small jar, it had quite a reputation. If you had any aches or pains, sore muscles, head cold, chest infection, in fact just about any minor ailment, just rub on a little Tiger Balm and the problem would go away, the punch line, this stuff worked. Whether real or just psychosomatic I don't know however I did take to carrying a small jar of Tiger Balm around with me for years.

After ten days 'holidaying' in Singapore they came looking. I was required back at Colerne in England. I was on an aeroplane that same night that would take me all the way. Ok, I guess I had squeezed it about as far as it could be squeezed. The aeroplane turned out to be a 24 Squadron Hastings that was passing through. 'Found you! Where have you been? back at Colerne they seem to think you've done a vanishing act.'

It was this hospitalisation in Singapore that made me promise myself that nothing, absolutely nothing, would ever cross my lips again in Karachi.

Around this time I bought another car. I had gone eight months without wheels ever since I disposed of the old Morris Eight at Dishforth. This time it was a fairly mature Vauxhall Velox. It leaked oil like all good English cars do and it had to live outside the mess in the snow and rain. It was all right, but when it came to negotiating the hill down into Bath in the snow and ice then it was not so good and getting back up the hill late at night could be a real problem but it was a car and a car is pretty important.

Colerne had a Station Flight equipped with a Chipmunk, an Anson and a Meteor. At this stage of my career I was not qualified to fly the Meteor, but I was checked out on the Chipmunk. I was right into it, I flew the Chipmunk at every opportunity, plenty of aerobatics and general running around the countryside. The Anson was a different story. I was not qualified, but the fellow in charge of the Station Flight was an Anson Instructor. Trying to nail him down for a bit of instruction was not easy. The Anson was an old twin engined plane, not that easy to fly so a bit of instruction was definitely required. I persevered but I never did get much dual. Finally at about the time I finished on 24 Squadron I managed to get checked out on the Anson, but after that I never had an opportunity to fly one again, there were not many of them left in service in the RAF.

Early in 1958 I heard about a jet refresher course at RAF Worksop up near Nottingham, I made inquiries. It was designed for jet-trained pilots who were not currently flying jets, that's me! I applied and surprise, without further ado I was back in the cockpit of a Vampire. It only lasted for a month, but I managed 20 hours of real flying in a Vampire 9. This whet my appetite and reminded me why I had travelled to England from New Zealand, I really did want to fly jets. The refresher was soon over and it was back to 24, paratroop dropping, boring!

Let me describe what's involved in paratrooping. It was a major role for 24, we were always doing it when not off overseas. The centre of activity was a place called Abingdon, an RAF Station near Oxford. We would fly over there, load up with army paratroops, then fly to nearby Salisbury Plain for the actual drop. The aircraft would position itself quite low and slow approaching the area where the drop was to happen. There were some coloured lights down the back which let the troops know just how close to the drop point we were. They went through various stages of preparedness then when we thought the aircraft was at the right spot we flicked the appropriate coloured light switch and the troops all jumped out through the big side door in quick succession. The idea was to do the drop from a low height so the troops were only in the air for the shortest possible time. For a pilot it was all pretty boring stuff, for a co-pilot, really boring. As I mentioned we seemed to do a lot of this when we were in England so it was very desirable to get off down the route to Australia whenever possible.

In May 1958 I was off on another detachment to Christmas Island. This time it was with the exchange crew from New Zealand, they still did not have a co-pilot. I assured them I was not yet the complete pom and we would get on just fine. We set off on the long journey through the Middle East, Far East, Australia, the Pacific, and eventually Christmas Island. This detachment did not go according to plan. The trip out took twelve days, we flew every day, accrued 74 hours flying time and suffered the trots in Karachi. When we arrived at Christmas there was no let up, three quick trips to Honolulu, then back down through the Pacific to Amberley in Queensland, then Edinburgh Field in South Australia. Edinburgh Field was the support airfield for the nuclear testing that had been going on at Maralinga in South Australia. A day at Edinburgh, then we retraced our steps to Christmas Island. Back at Christmas we got lucky and had a week off, we needed it, the flying had been intense with no breaks. We enjoyed our week, swimming, lying in the sun, playing with the crabs and a couple of exploratory trips into the island's interior. This was fascinating, the terrain was rough with big lumps of ancient coral all over the place, and the crabs, all 120 million of them, the whole place seemed to move as we crashed our way through the undergrowth, it was the crabs. The island's centre was dominated by a large brackish salt water swamp, not a very hospitable place. There were coconut palms everywhere, big mature ones, probably around fifty years old at this stage and still producing plenty of crab food.

Crab holes were everywhere, some were seriously big, we wondered just how big some of these crabs were. We soon satisfied our curiosity about the interior, it was not much of a place, lying in the sun down by the beach had it all over exploring. Our little holiday on Christmas came to an end, off to Edinburgh Field again, this time our luck ran out. On the first leg, Christmas to Canton, then on to Nandi, we experienced a propeller problem resulting in an engine shut down. We landed at Nandi on three engines and remained there for several days, very enjoyable days, while spare parts were rustled up. Then it was off to Amberley, When we got to Amberley our newly repaired propeller was not quite up to scratch, some more work was required to get it right. An air test was necessary after the servicing and this opened up some opportunities. We got airborne, determined that the offending propellor was ok, then enjoyed an hour or so flying around having a look at the immediate area. We flew inland to a farming area called Darling Downs, we were quite low and this gave us a magnificent view of the countryside, large tracts of open ground mixed in with intensively cultivated areas, we saw a lot of kangaroos on this open land. This was new to me, I had never seen a kangaroo. Our low flying Hastings frightened them and it was quite a sight watching all these kangaroos bounding along. We continued flying around Darling Downs having a good look at what appeared to be quite an intensively farmed area, then back to Amberley. Next morning off to Edinburgh Field, more bad luck, an engine failure going into Edinburgh, more time off. We put this to good use having a look around nearby Adelaide. One of the resident Australian pilot's at Edinburgh, a Meteor jet jock, took us under his wing and suggested we might like to come along to his friend's flat and meet the flatmates. The friend was a rather spectacular Australian girl who was a student at the local airline hostess training facility operated by TAA, Trans Australian Airlines, and yes, you guessed it, the three flatmates were all fellow students. We had a good time with these girls, my first time back with people who thought like me, well almost, Australians are pretty close. At this stage of my life I had been away from New Zealand for two and a half years. Our run of luck, you could call it good or bad, continued. The aeroplane was fixed and we were off on the long trip back to Christmas. Straight away another engine failed and we returned to Edinburgh, more time off. Then it all changed completely, the crew was split up, our aircraft was taken off us. I guess three engine failures in quick succession was not viewed very well by someone further up the line but you can hardly blame the operating crew for engineering failures. I spent three weeks at Edinburgh Field then I was crewed up with another 24 Squadron aircraft that was returning to the UK. We flew from Edinburgh to Darwin, spent the night there, then on to Changi where things got messy again, our aircraft was taken from us, required for more important duties. We had a week to wait for a replacement so we used this time having a look around Singapore, I was the tour guide, I now knew a bit about the place.

RAF Changi was huge in the 1950s, the main British military base in the Far East. The airfield supported numerous military facilities and there was a large British presence. Today Changi is the site of Singapore's International Airport. In the 1950s several RAF transport squadrons were based there and right next door was Changi village. I had been in the village before, on this occasion we spent some time enjoying all that it had to offer, it's a fascinating place. The main activity was catering to the needs of British service personnel based at Changi. Walk along the main street and the pressure's on, everything imaginable was on sale, the pressure to buy intense. Personal tailoring was big business. I don't think anyone who passed through the village came away without having a garment of some sort specially tailored, just for them. Good eating was readily available and a particularly good place was a collection of food stalls just beyond the village next to Changi jail. All sorts of kebabs, prawn balls, sweet and sour, everything Asian was available, it was a popular spot.

Eventually a replacement Hastings arrived and off we went, different route this time. First stop Karachi, the trots again, then Khormaksa in Aden, a place new to me, then a swing through Africa; Nairobi, Entebbe and Kano in Nigeria. These places were all new experiences. For some reason that I don't recall, we had a day off in Nairobi. Eastleigh is the airfield there, we parked our Hastings at Eastleigh and proceeded to enjoy our day off in East Africa. It was suggested we might like to go on a truck trip into the local game park, Nairobi National, there was a trip organised for that day, 'yes please we would love to.' Off we went in the back of a big truck that was covered with a steel mesh cage to see some African wild life. We were not disappointed, Giraffes, Water Buffalo, Zebras, Wildebeests, Hippopotamuses, plenty of Monkeys, Crocodiles and a pride of Lions, a spectacular animal show which we thoroughly enjoyed until our adventure took an unfortunate turn, the truck broke down. There was much activity trying to get it going again without success, the day was drawing to a close as well, this could be different, it was. Darkness enveloped us and the night creatures came out to have a look, bit like a Hollywood movie. There were all these pairs of eyes visible in the dark which was rather spooky, then there were some animal noises, very spooky. We huddled inside our steel cage, we were certainly not going anywhere. Eventually the cavalry arrived, another truck, it was about midnight when we finally got going. I still remember all those eyes looking at us that night. I never did determine just what sorts of creatures they belonged to. Next morning we set off for Entebbe in Uganda. Entebbe is on the shores of Lake Victoria in the middle of Africa, right on the equator, 5000 feet up. Because of the elevation the place enjoys a perfect climate. Along both sides of the airport runway were a lot of big anthills, these things were around five feet high, hard as concrete, you would not want to run off the runway at Entebbe. Later in my RAF career I was to get to know this place well. On this occasion however we did not get beyond the airport, it was a straight refuelling stop, then off to Kano, another interesting experience. Kano, in the north of Nigeria is a place where there's a lot of strife between Muslims and Christians and between people from the north and those from the south. Something that did impress me, all the big brightly coloured lizards, they were everywhere, it took a bit of getting used to. We spent a night in the town but it was not exactly a fun place, a collection of mud huts and a lot of big lizards. From there it was Idris again then back to Lyneham in England and would you believe an engine failed going into Lyneham. I had been away three months, experienced four engine failures, flown with two different crews, spent several weeks in Adelaide, had enjoyed interludes at Nandi and Singapore, but had not spent much time actually on Christmas Island. The imprest, yes I had one and by the time I got back to Colerne I really could not track all the spending which had gone through it, could be a long session with the Accounts Officer. Some of the places we visited on that trip back to England were to feature again in my life.

I was having a great time on 24 Squadron, certainly seeing a lot of the world but where was it leading. I was very young and had no real flying experience. My co-pilot role on a Hastings was not exactly advancing my flying career and the expectation of becoming a jet jock had virtually disappeared. Because of the RAF's downsizing there were a lot of pilots around and very few flying positions so my co-pilot role was not so bad, all things considered. The one unusual aspect was my age. Up until that time pilots had joined Transport Command well on in their flying careers after they had accumulated a lot of experience, it was certainly required. I, and several other young fellows, had joined straight off a wings course, a situation that had not occurred before in Transport Command, there was this lack of experience problem. In the normal course of events a co-pilot could expect to advance and become a captain however this required a lot of flying experience, including a lot of actual aircraft handling. We were certainly getting plenty of experience, but not quite the type that was required to advance a flying career, as for aircraft handling, zilch, we were not even allowed to do landings or take offs in a Hastings, we did do it, but not officially. I raised the matter with the boss one day, he admitted he could not see where we were going either. There was talk about taking some of us in a year's time or so and turning us into captains. Hmm, I could not see that happening, we were just not getting the aircraft handling that would be required. It was around this time that I firmed up my decision to leave the RAF at the eight year point and enter civil aviation. I had seen the type of flying the airlines were enjoying out in the Pacific, that was for me.

Life seldom follows the path you envision and in my case things took a real turn for the better. Eventually I managed to do all the things that I wanted so much; jet jock, and in one of the most desirable flying roles in the RAF, then flying around the Pacific in big jets.

Having made the decision to leave the Air Force I checked around to see what was available to facilitate the move. I discovered the Air Force was very generous in providing for people to advance their general education by allowing them to attend various courses available out in the civil community. Umm! I am going to be leaving the RAF in a few years, *I have decided!* I will need a commercial pilots license for starters, what's available? It turned out a very good commercial pilots licence course was available in London at the Sir John Cass College, what's more if you went on this course the RAF would pay the bills, really. The upshot was me moving into the Officers Mess at Biggin Hill, a famous World War

Two Spitfire base on the outskirts of London. Each morning I commuted into the city and attended the Sir John Cass College, another interesting period in my early life. I commuted into the city on the local train with all the good suburban citizens, got off, walked across London Bridge, along the edge of the Thames, past the Billingsgate fish market, phew did it smell, and continued on to the school. Late in the afternoon I did the same trip in reverse, I even purchased a black umbrella, it's good form to conform. This went on for six weeks. There was an interesting cross section of people on this course, a BOAC type doing an ALTP, that's an Airline Transport Pilots Licence, some Middle Eastern fellows who wanted commercial licences like me, a wealthy young chap who thought it would be fun to be a pilot, well yes, a girl who wanted to be an airline pilot, and a Cathay pilot who needed an ALTP; I should explain here that this course was fairly small with plenty of individual instruction, it covered both a commercial licence and the more advanced ALTP. After an enjoyable six weeks of being a London suburban commuter I sat the exam, bit different! The Battersea Town Hall was the venue, a huge cavernous place. About two hundred candidates turned up, some dodgy characters, plenty of cheating, some pretty desperate people. There seemed to be two types of candidate, those who came prepared, and those who didn't. The upshot of it all was a shiny new UK Commercial Pilot's Licence, something I was to put to good use in a few years time. At the end of this episode I returned to Colerne, more paratrooping, boring.

Not long after this a day trip to Germany came up, a troop drop on an airfield called Geilenkirchen. Off we went and landed at RAF Geilenkirchen, a NATO airfield that was part of the Second Tactical Air Force in West Germany. Lined up on the tarmac was a squadron of Canberra B(I)8 interdictor aircraft, 59 Squadron. The interdictor role was generally regarded as the best flying job in the air force and the twin jet Canberra B(I)8 just about the hottest thing around. I was very impressed. There and then I made one of life's decisions, *I am going to get myself onto 59 Squadron.*

It was after this trip that I began to realise if I wanted to achieve my ambition to become a jet jock I would have to *make* it happen. It was also around this time that I got some fatherly advice from a senior officer at Colerne about how you get what you want in this man's air force, you ask for it and don't take no for an answer. I wrote to the powers that be and told them I wanted to do a Canberra conversion and then be posted to 59 Squadron at Geilenkirchen, it happened, but it didn't happen right away.

In August 1958 I went to America. I had spent time in Hawaii but I had never been to mainland America. Later in my life I was to see a lot of the States, I even got to live there, however in 1958, at the tender age of 21, it was all new and exciting. We were to deliver some nuclear material to March Air Force Base in California and again it was the all New Zealand crew. I have often thought about that, why us for some of these more unusual tasks. At the time we were all young and bullet proof, it did not get a second thought however, I did think back to that gun running episode, the all New Zealand crew. Off we went to RAF Aldergrove in Northern Ireland. I have mentioned that the Hastings was not noted for its range and Aldergrove was as close as we could get to North America before having to cross the North Atlantic. Next stop, Goose Bay in Canada. What an experience, snow and ice everywhere, and cold, like you would not believe. It was here that I encountered French Canadians for the first time. The barman in the mess at Goose Bay was a fiery fellow who kept talking in French. Being an ignorant colonial it was all a bit strange to me until a Canadian fellow, who had had a few, enlightened me that the barman was a French Canadian, he then gave me a thorough briefing on French Canadians. I don't think he was very well disposed towards them. From Goose we flew to Offutt AFB in Nebraska, what a change. From snow and ice to corn, as far as the eye could see, corn, and dead flat, not a bit of high ground anywhere, we were in the corn belt in midwest America. Offutt was headquarters for SAC, Strategic Air Command. The sight that greeted us was astounding; there were huge B47 bombers everywhere, hundreds of them. That evening we were accommodated in the Officers Mess at Offutt, what a fascinating experience, you could just sense the power of the place. The American officers in the mess appeared to be a different breed as well, very sharp capable people. At the time there must have been enough nuclear capability at Offutt to destroy the world several times over. The following day we set off for March AFB in California, and again, what a sight, the place was crowded with more B47s, how many of these aircraft were there. At the time the Cold War's opposing nuclear forces were engaged in a massive build up of military might, this was one visible result. Little did I know it then, but in eighteen months time I was to be an integral part of this nuclear deterrent. We did not have long at March, an overnight stay then back to Offutt, Goose Bay, and across the North Atlantic to England. I had been to America, I was very impressed.

The stop at Offutt was to pick up a senior RAF Officer who had just finished an exchange posting at SAC Headquarters. It turned into quite a show. All set to depart and this fellow had not appeared then across the tarmac which was covered with all these huge B47s, a very shiny Cadillac convertible appears driven by a female, a very attractive female. Out hops our senior RAF fellow who then proceeds to say his farewells to his lady friend, only in America, it was a very 'steamy' goodbye with thousands looking on. We did not see much of this fellow during the trip back to England which included a stop at Goose Bay, he slept all the way. Years later I witnessed a similar performance on the tarmac at the old Payer Lebar airport in Singapore. I was piloting a DC8, all set to go, one passenger missing, no aerobridges in those days, you walked across the tarmac. The missing passenger arrives in a sports car, across the tarmac. It was a Cathay Pacific pilot in uniform, with a pretty girl. He proceeds to give a very public display of his affection for this girl then bounds up the steps into our DC8 and sleeps all the way to Sydney.

In April, 1959, not long before I left 24 Squadron, we did a trip out through all the usual places to Australia again. This time we went to Maralinga in South Australia. Maralinga was the site of some extensive nuclear testing which was carried out by the British in the 1950s, the subject of much controversy. Not much there, empty desert as far as the eye could see. We dropped our load and continued on to Edinburgh Field near Adelaide where we enjoyed a day off. No, the girls were no longer in the flat, they had moved on. Back to Darwin and this time we had six days off. Don't recall just why, I do remember the time we spent there though. Darwin seemed like a frontier town in the 50s, big pubs, bat wing doors, very noisy drinkers, bit like Ipswich near Brisbane. Very wide streets, apparently you had to be able to turn a bullock cart around in the width of the street, honestly, that's what the locals told us. We were accommodated in the Officers Mess at the Australian Air Force base, very comfortable, careful in the toilets, those toads. One day we organised a trip to a place called Berry Springs, about an hour's drive inland. A popular swimming and picnicking area, a delightful place. Plenty of bush and crystal clear water. What we did not know was this was crocodile country, there were crocodiles around. At the time, the late 1950s, crocodiles had been hunted almost to extinction in the Darwin area, the risk of attack was considered negligible. I did notice in the paper the other day, now more than 50 years on, there had been a fatal crocodile attack at Berry Springs, interesting. After that enjoyable interlude we set off back to England along the now familiar route, this time we refuelled at Khartoum in the Sudan, another new experience and a place I was going to be seeing again.

In the middle of June 1959 I did my last trip with 24 Squadron. I had been posted to RAF Strubby to do a jet refresher course on Meteors to be followed by a conversion course onto Canberras. When I heard this you could have knocked me over with a feather, that letter I had written some months earlier *demanding* a Canberra conversion and a posting to 59 Squadron had worked, the advice was good. This final Hastings trip was to be a one week sweep through Africa that would get me back to Colerne with about a week left to pack my bags and get to Strubby, jets at last. Off we went, Idris, a place I was going to see a lot in the future, then Kano, Entebbe, Khormaksar, then back to Entebbe and that's where everything changed, the Hastings broke down, we were still at Entebbe six days later. Suddenly this was a big problem, it was now June 23rd, the Strubby course started on the 29th. I had bad memories of arriving late from New Zealand for a wings course a few years earlier. From Entebbe we were scheduled to go to Kano again, then Idris, Lyneham, and Colerne, three days flying, life was taking a potentially disastrous turn.

There was a magnificent hotel at Entebbe located right on the edge of Lake Victoria, we did not stay there however, but at a lesser hotel in nearby Kampala the capital of Uganda. The Lake Victoria Hotel did not escape my notice however. So here I was, stuck in Africa, a callow youth on the crew of this big RAF transport plane that had broken down, all I wanted was to be out of the place. The Hastings was fixed and on the 25th we got airborne for Kano. I arrived back at Colerne two days later, some fast packing and off to Strubby, phew, made it, I was going to be a jet jock at last.

My posting was to an all weather jet refresher course flying meteors. I was 22 years old. The idea was to bring me up to speed on jets before doing the Canberra conversion at Basingbourne, an RAF station near Cambridge. Good idea, I had enjoyed a fantastic two years on 24 but I was not exactly a practising jet jock. A week after arriving at Strubby I was zipping around in a Meteor 7 being instructed in how to do it all and a week after that, I was doing it solo in a Meteor 8. It was an intense two months of Meteor flying. At the end of August I had completed the course, 50 hours of flying on real jets, I was up to speed, where's the Bassingbourne posting? Where indeed was the Bassingbourne posting? It was to be four long months before it arrived. It was a bad time for me, had I blown it somewhere, would I ever see B(I)8s and Geilenkirchen. I subsequently found out the delay was indeed brought about by my own actions. I had virtually demanded 59 Squadron in my original request to get out of Transport Command however there were no vacancies occurring at the right time at Geilenkirchen, I had to wait, it's just they never tell you these things. I acquired a Zephyr Six car at Strubby, the Vauxhall I had at Colerne had died some months earlier. The Zephyr proved to be an opportune buy because I had to cool my heals at Strubby from the end of August until the posting arrived four months later and I finally went off to Bassingbourne, the car was a useful asset during this period. Altogether I spent six months at Strubby, right through the summer of 59, that summer was one out of the book, England at its best. I was not the only keen young pilot getting the run around with postings, there were another couple of fellows destined for Javelin all weather fighter squadrons, their circumstances similar to mine, no postings. Strubby was being used as a holding point for pilots and this apparently did not go down too well with the people running the flying at Strubby. Their approach was, we had completed the refresher course that was it, no further Meteor flying for us. Having been brought up to speed we were now going to fall behind again, not good! The Strubby people were adamant, no more flying. I think we were caught in a power play between the Air Ministry people in London and the operational people at Strubby, what to do with pilots waiting for postings. Well the weather was fantastic, warm and sunny, so we took to enjoying ourselves in the local countryside. Strubby was right on the coast in the eastern part of Lincolnshire near a town called Mablethorpe, a local attraction was a big sandy North Sea beach. We went to the beach a lot during that summer but by my standards it was not the

Meteor 8

greatest. It was backed up by an area of sand hills, which was great, the downside was the oil, the beach was contaminated. A swim in the North Sea, which was not that warm, usually resulted in a few greasy patches on the body, the sand had a lot of tar like goo mixed into it as well, but it was a beach and we enjoyed it, perhaps I was being a bit too critical. Then there were the pubs. The area around

Strubby was blessed with plenty of excellent pubs, we patronised them all, frequently. The enforced holiday at the beach was starting to look up. With all this time off we got to know a few of the locals, usually girls and we found ourselves having a pretty good time. The Zephyr was suddenly a great asset, our social lives definitely took a turn for the better. We took to organising evening BBQs and bonfires amongst the sand hills behind the beach, we had a great time. There was a Butlins Holiday Camp nearby at Skegness, something new to me, nothing like it in New Zealand. One day we went over and investigated, certainly different, a sort of regimented holiday where you will enjoy yourself, or else. There was a beauty parade by the pool, enormously popular with the residents, this was followed by numerous games where everyone had to take part and it was all supervised by staff running around in red uniforms who were called Redcoats; different!

I was becoming very concerned about the lack of flying during this waiting period, I made inquiries about what, if anything, was available. Yes, there was something available, Chipmunk flying at Ternhill. Chipmunks? I had jets in mind. My life was taking an all too familiar turn again however I was not going to let an opportunity slip by. RAF Ternhill was a big flying school similar to the one at Feltwell where I had flown Provosts several years earlier, they were hosting a Combined Cadet Force, or CCF, summer camp for students. They required some pilots to give the cadets air experience and it was to be done in Chipmunks, ok, count me in. Off I went to Ternhill where I spent ten days flying young cadets around in the back of a Chipmunk, pretty boring stuff however to see the looks of appreciation on their young faces was reward enough. There was one moment of drama that one lucky cadet was able to share with me, we had an engine failure. As luck would have it we were right over the airfield at Ternhill when it occurred. There was a loud bang, the engine stopped and the windscreen was suddenly covered with oil.

We circled down without an engine and landed, not a problem, there was one young lad with a real story to tell. After Ternhill that was it, no more flying, I was going to be a bit rusty when, and if, I started the Canberra conversion.

One of the staff at Strubby, a Flight Lieutenant navigator of Indian extraction was well known for his cooking. It had become a regular event that on a Sunday he would take over the mess kitchen and produce a curry for lunch. His Sunday curry had become very popular, it was right up there with the best and people would turn up from far and wide to enjoy this event, forty plus diners was not unusual. The RAF Flying College, a place where senior officers went to do advanced flying courses, was at nearby RAF Manby, many of these people would turn up at Strubby for the Sunday curry. It was a hot one, a lot of beer was required. I have happy memories of extended Sunday lunches in the warmth of that summer at Strubby becoming overheated and rather intoxicated in the company of some quite senior officers who were also getting into a similar state, very enjoyable.

A posting, at last. My summer holiday came to an abrupt end which was rather timely, the glorious summer of 59 was drawing to a close, winter was setting in, the east coast of Lincolnshire is no place to be during an English winter. A few days before Christmas 1959 I drove the Zephyr down to Bassingbourne near Cambridge to finally realise my dream, I was going to be a real jet jock at last.

The Bassingbourne course was big. Day one we all gathered together in one large room, pilots and navigators all in together. An instructor announced that we were to team up, one pilot and two navigators, which is how a Canberra was crewed. Most of the people on this course would finish up on conventional bomber squadrons, except me, I was quietly confident I was destined for B(I)8s, I did not have it in writing but I was quite sure it was going to happen. There was an anomaly here because the B(I)8 version of the Canberra only has one navigator. The Bassingbourne course did not cater for this, very few people were lucky enough to get onto one of the three B(I)8 squadrons in Germany, I hope they know I'm destined for B(I)8s. It was a bit awkward, nobody knew anybody else. We were all standing around looking at each other with all sorts of thoughts going through our heads. I am not sure how Harry and I teamed up but team up we did and Harry Scarff turned into a very good friend indeed. A second navigator was required and John Briggs joined us. Again I cannot really remember how we found each other but we did, we formed a three man crew for the course. During our time at Bassingbourne it soon became apparent that Harry and I were well matched, I thought I had better do something to ensure that it would be Harry who would be posted to Geilenkirchen with me when we finished the course. Nothing like being overconfident. I approached higher authority and made my request known. It fetched a rather curious response about how did I know that my posting would be to B(I)8s. At graduation, surprise surprise Harry and I were posted to No:59 Squadron at Geilenkirchen in Germany on B(I)8s, that advice a year or so earlier had been good. John Briggs went to a squadron at Wildenrath, also in Germany, tragically he was killed a short time later in a Canberra crash.

The conversion at Bassingbourne was quite intense, first we had to learn how to fly the Canberra, then get ourselves up to all weather combat standard. Additional pressure came from the very good social facilities on offer in the nearby university town of Cambridge, a young lad just had to take advantage of that. Careful management of available energy resources was required, people did fail this course. An additional distraction was the closeness of London and an excellent rail link to get there. Some of the characters on our course had 'connections' in London, off we went to the big smoke on several weekends and thoroughly enjoyed ourselves. Mondays could be difficult. We progressed through the course and made it to graduation. The postings were announced, Harry and I were a bit like the cat that got the cream. Harry advised he was going to drive over to Geilenkirchen in his Morris Minor. I still had the Zephyr Six but it was becoming a bit 'used,' not really worth taking to Germany. We heard that used cars in Germany were relatively cheap and usually pretty good. There was a two week break before we were required to appear at Geilenkirchen so I took the Zephyr down to London and checked into the Overseas Visitors Club the idea being to sell the Zephyr. The OVC, as the club was known, was a colonial hang out run by South Africans. They operated a string of rental flats in the Kings Cross area for club members, the place was very popular. I found myself in a flat with a hard case Rhodesian chap, a gorgeous South African girl, and a couple of NZ girls. It was an enjoyable two weeks, and yes, I did manage to sell the car. Then some fond farewells to my newfound friends and off I went to Germany in the train.

59 Squadron Geilenkirchen – Germany

I arrived at a small nondescript railway station in Germany one April morning in 1960, Geilenkirchen, just north of Aachen, right on the border with Holland. When the RAF posted you somewhere you were given a railway ticket and a date to be there. I was twenty-three years old about to realise my dream, a fully-fledged jet jock in one of the most sought after roles in the Air Force, 59 Squadron, a B(I)8 strike outfit. Harry was driving over in his car, a Morris Minor, something that could make him pretty popular. We were about to be on the frontline of the Cold War, something we did not quite realize at the time. Our primary role, tactical nuclear strike using the recently developed LABS system. A significant secondary role was low level interdiction. LABS was short for low altitude bombing system, it was a way of delivering a tactical nuclear bomb onto a target without the enemy even knowing you were coming and, hopefully, without killing yourself in the process, however, as we were about to find out, although you may not actually kill yourself you could come perilously close to achieving just that. The Canberra aircraft we would be flying for the next three years was an extraordinary aeroplane, originally conceived as a conventional bomber, the design proved to be so successful that it was adapted for many other roles. One of these was low-level interdiction, which means attacking the enemy's supply lines and generally disrupting his forces on the ground in the immediate area of a battle. The RAF had four of these interdictor squadrons, they constituted part of the UK's contribution to NATO's Second Tactical Air Force, or 2TAF as it was known, based in West Germany. The interdiction role was secondary however, the B(I)8s primary task was tactical nuclear strike. They formed part of a quick reaction force that would be amongst the first to strike back should the West ever be attacked in Europe. They, with the help of others, would destroy the Eastern Block's ability to wage war by knocking out all the airfields in Eastern Europe with tactical nuclear weapons and it would all be done at low level.

59 Squadron B(I)8s

The designation, B(I)8, was intended to describe the role that the aircraft had been designed for. The original Canberra that went into RAF service was a B2, there were a lot of B2 squadrons in the 1950s and early 60s. The B2 was a high level bomber hence the designation B, it was the second development model, hence the 2. All the B2s were eventually replaced with a later model, the B6. Our version of the Canberra was the eighth development model hence the 8, it was a bomber, which gave it the B, it was also fitted with all the interdiction gear, hence the (I). The squadron also had a two-seat training Canberra called a T4, it was the fourth Canberra development model. The original Canberra featured a rather restrictive cockpit canopy which became quite a handicap when flying at low level, this was replaced on the B(I)8 with a big fighter type bubble canopy that gave the pilot a much better unrestricted view. There was a nose cone observation position for one navigator, much of the navigation being low level map reading. The RAF had four of these interdictor squadrons in Germany, three equipped with B(I)8s, the fourth the original B(I)6 interdictor version, the basic difference being the B(I)6 had the original pilot's canopy not the new bubble one.

It was essential that we practised the skills required for low level interdiction and LABS, this meant low flying. For a pilot this was flying nirvana hence the popularity of the B(I)8s with pilots, for navigators I'm not so sure. Lying prone jammed up in the nose cone looking at the ground going by frighteningly fast just a few feet away was not my idea of fun, there was not much a navigator could do about it either, the pilot had all the controls.

59 Squadron had a compliment of twelve pilots and twelve navigators. Most of the pilots had completed at least one operational tour on front line jets, mainly high altitude Canberra bomber squadrons, they were experienced. There were a couple of younger chaps on their first operational tour, career fellows from the RAF College at Cranwell. It was apparent that most of these pilots were well prepared for the demands imposed on them in this nuclear strike role. The career chaps from Cranwell were being thrown in at the deep end to see if they could hack it, give them an opportunity to prove themselves, see if they had *the right stuff;* then there was me. I was not quite sure just where I fitted in, it was not my first tour, but then you could hardly say I was experienced, well certainly not flying jets. Trundling around the world in a Hastings without being allowed to actually fly the thing was a rather unusual preparation for this elite flying role however here I was and I was going to make the most of this glorious opportunity.

Harry and I settled in and started the operational conversion program. There was a lot of learning to do before we would be entrusted with the responsibility, the huge responsibility, of being part of a nuclear strike squadron. We were both single and moved into the Officers Mess, I bought an old Volkswagen which let Harry off the transport hook. We soon struck up a friendship with a young Scotsman who also 'lived in,' Gordon Glennie. He was the station equipment officer, a real live wire. 23 years old, he had been a Cranwell graduate however colour blindness had cut short his flying ambitions, he was now pursuing a career on the ground, 'much safer' he reckoned. Gordon appeared to have a self-destruct gene in his make up, he was a complete tearaway, the three of us soon became very good friends.

To become operational on a front line squadron in 2TAF you had to be proficient in all the various methods by which your aircraft could strike at the enemy, in the case of the B(I)8 this was a formidable task. The aircraft was designed for the strike role, it could do this with devastating effect using a variety of weapons, we had to become proficient in the use of them all. When we arrived on the squadron we could fly the aircraft, that was all. We now had to learn how to carry out a LABS attack with a nuclear weapon, by day, and at night, how to dive bomb with conventional bombs, how to use the four 20mm Hispano cannon to take out ground vehicles and how to take low level reconnaissance photographs. The B(I)8 was also capable of air to ground rocket attack however this was put on the back burner, there was just not enough time to practise all these skills. Our primary role was tactical nuclear strike, this was our main focus and it occupied most of our time.

First up we had to be able to fly around low and fast without coming to grief so we had to practise the wonderful art of low flying. Harry learnt how to lie in the nose cone of a B(I)8 and map read, at speed, up close and personal and to deal with the sheer terror of it all something which never ceased to amaze me, how did he cope? We then started an intensive period of air to ground gunnery and dive bombing at Nordhorn, which was a bombing range not far from Geilenkirchen, when we had a handle on all that we flew out to Idris, an airfield near Tripoli in Libya, a place I had been to with 24 Squadron, there we used the Tarhunah range out in the desert. This was in the days before Gadaffi when Libya was a friendly country. When we had mastered all these interdiction skills it was back to Germany where we were introduced to LABS.

LABS involved flying the aircraft at high speed towards a target at very low level then at a predetermined point pull up into the start of a loop. As the aircraft is going up into the loop the bomb is automatically released and is tossed up and away, ahead of the aircraft. At the top of the loop the idea was to roll out and speed off in the direction you had just come from attempting to put as much distance as possible between you and the nuclear blast which would be occurring shortly after. The scary part was because we were an all weather strike squadron we were expected to be able to do this in all weather, both day and night. Low flying at night, they'd not told us about that, suddenly some of the glow was fading.

We carried out our first LABS manoeuvres at altitude, then as we became proficient the level was lowered until we could do it, at speed, from ground level, and with considerable accuracy. This emphasis on accuracy was a moot point. The idea was to put a crater in the enemy airfield's runway, we had this bomb that would do the job, an American nuclear weapon called a Mark 7 B28, it had the explosive power of 70,000 tons of TNT, I guess some accuracy was required. We could toss this bomb a considerable distance ahead of us and place it within 30 yards of the target. During the whole of this work up period we did a lot of low flying, we were also introduced to the dubious art of low flying at night, the night bit never did appeal. All this soon used up the six months that had been allocated to become fully proficient, in October 1960 we were declared operational. I had achieved my dream, I was now a fully-fledged operational jet jock, a real *Cold War Warrior*, but it had taken a long time to get there, five and a half years. I had just turned 24.

Life at Geilenkirchen was great, plenty of low flying, all legal. Readers who are not familiar with flying may not appreciate the significance of this. Flying an aeroplane close to the ground is an absolute adrenaline rush, pilots love it. Civilian populations around the world however are not impressed by noisy aeroplanes speeding by at low level and in most places all sorts of restrictions have been put in place to prevent it. In Germany, in the early 1960's, the NATO forces had mapped out vast areas of the northern part of the country as designated low flying areas where their Air Forces could practice low flying because that was how, and probably where, the next war was going to be contested. The local population must have cursed us. We spent the majority of our flying time roaring around this northern part of what was then West Germany, just as low as we could go at anything up to 330 knots. The Canberra was a noisy aeroplane and at speed, just 50 feet or less over your house, it must have been hell. Well that is what we did, it was legal and boy did we enjoy it. There was a downside however, the margin for error was not great and we were required to do it at night as well. You cannot see at night, a fundamental fact for the human species, we soon realised that low flying at night was just silly stuff. That's the way it was however, the planners had decreed that our role was to be able to strike at any time, war does not just happen during daylight hours, so go and practice low flying at night.

It was around this stage of my life that I first started to think about why front line combatants were so young, it's all very exciting, a lot of fun when you are young, keen, and bulletproof, nothing's going to happen to you. There was the occasional fatal accident amongst the

NATO Air Forces in Europe, I remember reflecting on the fact that really we were considered expendable. We were a front line fighting force, an attrition rate had to be expected, low flying at night was certainly not improving our chances. There were other things that we were required to do and whilst not thinking about it too much at the time, with hindsight some of these things should have been causing us concern, for instance, our target.

Our primary role was deep penetration tactical nuclear strike into the Warsaw Pact countries. The idea was to reduce the enemy's ability to strike at us, to achieve this we were going to knock out their airfields. An airfield is only as good as its runway, once that is rendered unusable then all the aircraft on that airfield are taken out of action. The best way of taking out a runway is to blast some big holes in it, however the bad guys will endeavour to fill in the holes and get back into action. In the early 1960s we had this American weapon that would make such a big hole that there would be precious little runway left, and the hole would be radioactive.

Harry and I were allocated a target and told to study it closely. We were to plan the complete operation from the time of getting airborne from Geilenkirchen, until we returned to Geilenkirchen, having taken out the target. When we had completed our planning we were to submit it to higher authority for approval. Plenty of maps and target photographs were supplied, and we were left to it. How some of these photographs had been obtained had us thinking. Our target airfield was on Poland's eastern border, a long way from Geilenkirchen. To get there, carry out the strike, and return, posed a problem, the Canberra did not carry enough fuel to do it all at low level. When this point was raised with the Intelligence Officer overseeing the planning his only advice was 'you figure it out.' The options were to go in at altitude, drop down to low level well before the target, carry out the strike, then return to altitude for the run back to Geilenkirchen. At altitude the Canberra's fuel consumption was much lower than at low level, consequently a much greater range was possible. The downside was that at altitude a B(I)8 would be a sitting duck. The B(I)8 was a strengthened version designed for low flying, it was a lot heavier than other Canberras, the extra weight reduced its high altitude performance. It appeared to us that the only way to get to the target intact was at low level, which is what we had been training for, it put us 'under the radar' making it very difficult for the bad guys to get at us. If we did this we could do the job but we would fall far short of Geilenkirchen when returning. This realization exercised our minds, made us wonder if this was intentional, were we expendable? The other thought was that while we were doing this, the other side would be doing the same thing to NATO's airfields in the west, it was probable that Geilenkirchen would have been reduced to a big hole in the ground. Harry and I pondered this dilemma long and hard and came up with our own unique solution, we would go low all the way, knock out our target airfield, then sit out the war on the beach at Bornholm, excuse me, Bornholm? Well there is a small Danish island in the Baltic well to the east of Denmark, called Bornholm, at the southeast corner there's a big sandy beach called Dueodde. We calculated that we could carry out our strike at low level then continue low level to Bornholm where we would land on this beach. We would have just enough fuel to do this. When we submitted our plan to the Intelligence Officer for approval we lied, we kept our Bornholm plan all to ourselves. It was beginning to dawn on us that if war occurred in Europe our survival chances were not good so a certain amount of self-preservation crept into our thinking. We decided to take a trip to Denmark, catch a ferry to Bornholm, and check out the beach. We really needed to know just how firm the sand was on Dueodde beach, it could influence the call on whether to make a wheels up or wheels down landing should we one day be called upon to make this terrible decision. We never did manage that trip to Bornholm.

Something else that we were required to do made us think long and hard about our survival chances. We were required to carry an eye shield, you know, one of those things that pirates with only one eye use in the movies. Should war occur in Europe there would be tactical nuke's going off all over the place. If you happened to be looking in the direction of one when it detonated then the flash would burn the retinas of your eyes, you would be blind. This would be catastrophic if you were piloting a jet at around three hundred knots at low level. To give you a chance the idea was to wear an eye shield over one eye. If you were unlucky and lost the exposed eye, not a problem, remove the eye shield and you would still have a good eye. You find this hard to comprehend? so did we! Taken to its logical conclusion we could be flying across Eastern Europe at low level, very fast, at night, with one eye covered. This was apparently what was expected. Nobody actually told us to go off and fly one eyed however we were given the eye shields and when we asked what they were for this was the story we got. I do not recall anyone actually practicing the art of one eyed flying and I really did wonder about how we would have coped should a shooting war have broken out in Europe.

Another thing that caused a bit of concern, the total lack of any means of defence should we be attacked. There was no defensive armament on the B(I)8, no radar jamming equipment, nothing at all. We did have one big advantage, our method of attack, fast and very low. When you think it through our ability to fly fast and low was a very effective defence. Attack from the ground by guns or missiles was rendered ineffective and attack from the air would be extremely difficult for the attacker in fact we were probably safer from attack than all the other higher flying aircraft.

Perhaps a word about what sort of scenario a war in Europe in the early 1960s would be like. Both sides, NATO in the West, the Warsaw Pact countries in the East, were heavily armed with tactical nuclear weapons. A tactical weapon is one that's used in the immediate theatre of conflict as opposed to a strategic weapon which is used to strike at the heartland of an opposing country. The explosive power of tactical nuclear weapons is usually expressed as the equivalent of so many thousands of tons of TNT, strategic weapons, so many millions. You can see from these figures the firepower involved is just so huge it becomes rather hard to comprehend. The bomb that we would be delivering onto a runway in Poland in the event of war had the explosive force of 70,000 tons of TNT, which is enormous.

NATO had four Tactical Air Forces in Europe all similarly armed, then there were large ground armies, many equipped with nuclear cannons. A nuclear cannon is a very big artillery weapon that fires a shell with a nuclear warhead. The total nuclear firepower that NATO had in position in Europe in the early 1960s was staggering. Add to this the Warsaw Pact's nuclear ability and it was pretty obvious that a war in Europe would have reduced the place to a nuclear wasteland.

During my time at Geilenkirchen I become fascinated by what had gone on during the Second World War in Germany. Here I was living in the place where it had all happened not that many years before. The aftermath was all around, war damage was evident everywhere. I particularly remember driving through nearby Duren not long after I arrived in Germany, the town was a ruin, it looked like something you saw in those old wartime pictures. There was a lot of recent history pertaining to Geilenkirchen as well. Hitler's Siegfried Line went through the place, right through Geilenkirchen village. During the pre-war years the Germans had extended and added to an old existing defensive line, their western wall, a line of fortifications first developed during World War One. This defensive line was a formidable barrier right along Germany's western border.

In the Geilenkirchen area the Siegfried Line consisted of an extensive system of bunkers, anti-tank barriers and other strong fortifications. In November 1944 the Allies arrived in the area and were confronted with the Siegfried Line. Operation Clipper was launched. The battle of Geilenkirchen took place between a combined British and American force and a strong German one. The Allies breached the Siegfried Line, the cost, 2000 casualties. It was where the allies first entered Germany. Many of the older locals had lived through that period and some of them were not favourably disposed towards 'Englanders.' There were a lot of large concrete bunkers around the place, most of them badly damaged, they had been left as they were at the end of the war. Most of the buildings in Geilenkirchen itself had been restored pretty much back to their original condition or else demolished and replaced with new ones, but not all, there were still a lot of severely damaged structures around; but let's get back to 59 Squadron.

There were plenty of things to occupy our off duty time. We were right on the border with Holland and we went across to Heerlen a small Dutch town that had a good bar and restaurant, the Kastalum, we were regulars. The restaurant part was in a 'picture postcard' cellar, the food, superb, oysters and large steaks, very popular with the local Dutch population. I will always remember these rather large Dutchmen with big bibs around their necks really enjoying a plate of oysters. The plate would be held high, the oysters slurped into the mouth with a bit down the bib, all done with a big smile on the face. Oysters were not my thing, I did not like them. I thought perhaps I could acquire the taste if I tried, they were obviously very enjoyable. Well I tried several times but no, just not me, damn! The steaks though were a different story, big, juicy and delicious. We downed many of them then one day our bubble was well and truly popped, we found out they were horsemeat, well it was very nice horsemeat. All this eating was accompanied by large quantities of beer, yep, Heerlen was a pretty good place.

Another popular spot was the Postwagen, a pub in Palenburg a small German village quite close to Geilenkirchen. We would descend on this place, usually late at night when we had been in the mess bar for far too long and were hungry. When beer was purchased at the Postwagen the waitress marked it up in groups of five on your beer coaster. The idea was that when you left you paid for the number of beers marked on your coaster. Well I guess it worked for the locals but unfortunately our lot were in the habit of firing these beer coasters around the place when we had drunk a few too many and that was pretty much always. The poor waitress would do her bun when this happened. The Postwagen was also known for its excellent half chicken and chips meal, 'ein halbes hahnchen und pommes frites' was what you asked for, very popular late at night. Eating 'halbes hahnchen' could become a bit of an ordeal however, especially if Gordon Glennie was around, he usually was. It had become a bit of one upmanship to nick some chips off your mate's plate however if it was noticed then you could expect a whack on the knuckles with a dinner knife. Now these dinner knives were usually pretty blunt, but not always, there was a fair incidence of cut fingers. Gordon, being a skinny Scotsman, was usually hungry, he always seemed to be involved in these antics. I'm not sure what the locals thought about these crazy Englanders eating half chickens and chips with blood dripping from cut fingers, very strange behaviour.

Our status in Germany in the 1960s, NATO military personnel, entitled us to certain tax exemptions, they were good. Petrol was purchased locally with vouchers that we got from military sources at a cheap tax-exempt price which was just as well because petrol was expensive. Liquor on the base at Geilenkirchen was cheap, then there was a big NAAFI, (Navy Army & Air Force Institute) store, again inexpensive. We also had access to the PX (Post Exchange) stores in the American zone to the south of Geilenkirchen. Just as well all these facilities were available to us, we did need some breaks, Air Force pay was not good. When you are young and on the high we were on, money did not seem to matter, but it was something you needed to finance the lifestyle, we were always broke.

When I arrived on 59 Squadron the CO was a hard-nosed South African Wing Commander who had seen service in the Second World War, a very experienced and good boss. One sunny Sunday he invited all the single aircrew around to his house for a BBQ, he also mentioned we would be able to meet a cousin who was visiting from London, umm, this could be interesting. The cousin turned out to be a very attractive South African girl doing her big OE, she was currently living in London. Her uncle, our boss, had invited her over to Germany to experience life on a front line jet base and experience a little of the Cold War atmosphere, she could meet some operational jet pilots as well, good build up eh! Well this attractive girl was way out of her comfort zone and all these lusty young pilots were giving her a lot of attention. She was quite a character and during the course of the afternoon I managed to get her London address and phone number. Later that evening, after an excellent day at the boss's place, he sent us all home, 'no you cannot take my cousin out tonight, no not even to the Postwagen, she's off back to London in the morning.' Crafty old dog, this girl had been at Geilenkirchen for a week, the boss had left it to the last day to 'show her,' he had us figured out. It did not end there though, I had to go to England in a week or so for a short course in London. I knocked on her door one afternoon and this young man answered, no she was not in, in fact she's away for a few days, what did you say your name was? I'll tell her you called, damn! It transpired that several other fellows had managed to get her details during that BBQ. During the next few months they had all managed to speak to the young man who answered her door in

London. It appeared she spent a lot of time being away for a few days. We figured the young man was the boyfriend and her largesse at Geilenkirchen had come back and bitten her on the bum. I remember her name was Roma, she had been a-roaming!

The Volkswagen I bought soon after arriving at Geilenkirchen was a good one, it was getting a lot of use and served me well until that fateful night towards the end of 1960 when my life took a turn for the worse. I was driving back to Geilenkirchen in the wee hours from across the border in Holland, when wham! whack! bam! the car, with me in it, was suddenly wrapped around a large tree at the side of the road; how did that happen? This incident was to cause me a lot of grief. In the course of whacking the tree I had also bowled a local farmer who had been walking along the road. Why was he out walking in the wee hours, yes well, why was I out driving? Fortunately he was not physically harmed however he was not happy and he definitely did not like Englanders. I could understand why it was that there was some resentment towards us. Here we were virtually an occupying force remember it was just fifteen years after the end of the war, it must have appeared that we had all the privileges, access to cheap petrol, patronising the pubs and restaurants, it probably looked like we had plenty of money, well that was wrong. We were young and healthy and always seemed to be intent on having a good time, which was correct. This did not go down too well with some of the locals, particularly the older people. I guess it was a hangover from the war, the Geilenkirchen area had suffered badly in that conflict and these people would have been living there at the time. The old fellow who had been hit by my car was very much a local, he had not been hurt but as far as he was concerned I should be strung up. The RAF Police from Geilenkirchen and the local German Police both got into the act, things began to look rather bleak for me. Apparently the politics of the situation were not in my favour. There had been numerous incidents involving cars, locals, and British Servicemen. The British authorities were quite good at looking after their own however there was a lot of resentment amongst the Germans about these sorts of incidents. It had been decided that there had to be an example made to appease the German authorities. Unfortunately for me I presented myself at just this time, what's more I was an Officer and a colonial, expendable, not good. Why did I think I was considered expendable? Well from the odd comment made by some senior British RAF Officers I got the impression that in some quarters it was thought that the colonials needed to be taken down a peg or two. The RAF was full of people from the colonies, particularly from New Zealand, in fact the further up the ranks you went in the RAF the more Kiwis you seemed to find holding senior positions. Then there was that gun running episode back on 24 Squadron, the New Zealand crew plus the ex-pat, all colonials again, expendable? My life took a nasty turn, higher authority decided that a court-martial, particularly that of an Officer, would probably appease the Germans, the British would be seen to be doing something about public relations. I was to be court-martialed at Geilenkirchen, the charge, dangerous driving. Geez I think I'm in big trouble!

What to do? I approached our Squadron Navigation Leader, a senior officer who I got on with really well, he was a bit of a bush lawyer. 'Sir, how about defending me, I think I am being a bit hard done by.' Why had the accident happened in the first place? Well it had been in the wee hours, a young lady had been involved, and I think it was just plain tiredness and inattention, certainly not dangerous, I guess that depends whose side you are on. 'Daddy Drake,' as our worldly-wise nav leader was affectionately known, agreed, 'yes they are making an example of you, not fair.' I think it was the involvement of a young lady that tickled his fancy. What had happened? I had been over in Heerlen, the Kastalum, where a young lady who I was rather keen on worked occasionally. When she finished work we visited a couple of bars together. I was on the way back to Geilenkirchen after dropping her off at her home in Heerlen when I had this accident. Why I had hit the tree I could not really recall. In the preamble to the court-martial we advised the prosecutor that the case would be defended, we were going to plead not guilty to the charge of dangerous driving, however we were prepared to plead guilty to a lesser charge of driving without due care and attention should this lesser charge be added to the charge sheet; sorry no deal. This was meant to be a showcase for the German authorities, I was meant to go down in a big way. We were advised that the trial was to proceed with just the one charge.

The Court Martial was held at Geilenkirchen and Daddy Drake proved to be a very effective advocate, he was able to make a good defence case from very little fact, we won, I was acquitted. This was not the way it was supposed to be, higher authority would not be happy. Fortunately for me I escaped to New Zealand on two months leave just after this trial. I heard later that higher authority was indeed not happy, their showcase trial had backfired badly, glad I was not around for a couple of months. I remember some sage advice from Daddy Drake after it was all over. 'Rex, you realize this can work to your advantage,' 'ah, no, enlighten me.' 'Well when your name comes up in the future, when career promotions and the like are being considered, you will not be just another name. The powers that be will remember you, the fellow that took them on and won, that can be a good thing.' I often think about that advice. It was never my intention to make a career in the Air Force in fact I was actively planning to leave at the end of my tour in Germany and return to New Zealand, I often wonder what could have been had I stayed on in the RAF. A couple of my mates from that time stayed on and rose to Air Marshal rank. I did not escape retribution entirely however. When I returned from New Zealand a couple of months later the RAF came up with a convoluted argument that I would not be allowed to drive in Germany for three months. I thought about it and decided not to push my luck, no driving for a while.

The Volkswagen which had been badly damaged in the accident was rebuilt by the local panel beater in Geilenkirchen village while I was away in New Zealand. When I returned I put it away in a garage that I had managed to get access to behind the Officers Mess, no driving for a while. Hang on, other people can drive my car, life does not have to be too restricted just because I'm not allowed to drive. It may cramp my style a bit, lots of nights out with the boys, oh well I guess that's the way it will be for a while. One of those nights out had an amusing sequel. I had returned to Geilenkirchen from New Zealand in the middle of a particularly severe winter, snow and ice everywhere. We had been to the Postwagen in the Volkswagen late at night, as I was not doing the driving I had had quite a few and I was not too fussed about putting the car back in the garage. It was left in the mess car park, that night it rained, freezing rain. Well the next morning, geez, what's happened to the car? It looked like a mound of ice welded to the ground. The freezing rain had completely coated the car with ice and moulded it to the car park. Not much I could do, wait for a thaw that fortunately happened later in the day, bit different!

Our circumstances in Germany placed us in a unique position that enabled us to take advantage of some tax concessions that various countries had in place at the time. Motor vehicles in particular attracted high taxes, however, there were ways of avoiding these. Both England and New Zealand had similar laws relating to motor vehicles, it was possible to use the law to your advantage, it worked like this. If you were resident outside your home country for a period of not less than two years and if you owned a new car for more than a year during that period then you could import it into your home country without having to pay any taxes. If you were a foreign resident in a country and you purchased a car, then providing you exported it out of that country after one year you would not have to pay any taxes on it in that country either. This meant that we were able to buy new cars tax free, drive them in Germany for at least a year, then return home to our country of residence with the car and not have to pay any taxes there either. A further stipulation was that you continue your ownership of the vehicle for a further two years before disposing of it. This opportunity just had to be taken advantage of. Money was a continuing problem, however, there were some good finance options available to servicemen wanting to buy tax free cars. Mercedes Benz were keen to sell to British servicemen. The thought of owning a brand new Merc was just irresistible. You had to be quick however, there was a long waiting list and I would have to own the vehicle for at least a year in Germany before I could take it back to New Zealand. I jumped in and ordered a brand new Mercedes 190S, to be picked up from the factory in Stuttgart in a few months time. Wow, wouldn't I cut a dash back in New Zealand! Shortly after I ordered the Merc another pilot on the squadron took delivery of an Austin Healy 3000, a pretty upmarket sports car, then another chap picked up an MG Sports. Gordon Glennie was really lucky, his parents bought him a new Daimler SP250, about the hottest sports car around at that time, me, well I was going to be the owner of a Mercedes 190 saloon, bit boring. The cost of the Merc was proving to be a bit much as well, even tax exempt they were not cheap. I looked around and decided that a young fellow really should have a sports car, a brand new Triumph TR3A was the thing for me, the price was right as well, however there was a problem. When you ordered from Mercedes, that was it, no pulling out. I cast around and found a keen young Army Officer who had left it too late to order a Merc, he would just love to take over my order, deal done, now for the TR3. The upshot of it all was me going to England during the summer of 1961 and taking delivery of a brand new TR3A, British racing green, wire wheels, overdrive, all the toys, at the factory in England. I drove it around England for a week visiting some old haunts then across the channel on the vehicular ferry, through France, Belgium and Holland, to Geilenkirchen. Now I was a member of 'The Club,' I had a real car!

The sports car club at Geilenkirchen took to visiting some of the European Grand Prix events that were contested at various venues not far from Geilenkirchen. The Belgium Grand Prix at Spa, the Dutch Grand Prix at Zandvoort, and the German one at the Nurburgring in the Eifel forest, all these places were close by. We had a great time going to these events and of course you had to take along a pretty girl to set the car off, make everyone envious. At the Nurburgring we were allowed to drive around the circuit when there was no racing, I took the opportunity to do just that in the TR3. Wow, what an experience, flat out on a steeply banked track, bit dodgy though. The German authorities must have thought so as well because not long after I did my circuit the old Nurburgring was closed and racing moved to Hockenheim. The Nurburgring was rebuilt and reopened again in 1985.

Who had the fastest car? Well I guess Gordon won on that count with his Daimler SP. It would do 140mph so that is what he did on the autobahns. We really needed to know just how fast our cars would go so we measured out a mile on the airfield runway at Geilenkirchen and carried out some timed runs. Gordon's Daimler, 141mph, the Austin Healy, 128mph. my TR3, 111mph, and the MG, 105mph. So now we had a pecking order. There was a young American Air Force Officer, Fred Maynard, living in the Mess at the time, he bought himself a Porsche 911, boy were we envious. The Porsche topped out at 109mph so that dropped him down the order a bit but wow, talk about road holding, the Porsche had us all whacked on that count. Tyres were a problem, they did not wear well. The autobahns were unrestricted, you could go as fast as you liked. My TR3 would do 111mph, so that's what I did. It had overdrive fitted so when I got up to speed I dropped into overdrive which lowered the engine RPM, then just maintained that speed mile after mile. The downside was tyre wear, you could just about see the rubber disappearing. In the early 1960s tyres were not designed for continuous high speed, if you did this the tyre wear was excessive. I used the latest Dunlop SP250 tyres which had very good road holding but were rather soft, they certainly suffered a high rate of wear.

Gordon's Daimler was popular, a rare sight in Germany, it attracted plenty of attention whenever he took it out. On one occasion some of the British girls who worked in the Embassy in Bonn, phoned the Mess at Geilenkirchen inquiring if any young British chaps would be interested in attending a party at the Embassy that night, there was a shortage of suitable men. Gulp, 'eh, yes, I'm sure that we can supply some keen young chaps.' 'Gordon, let's go.' Five of us piled into the Daimler, top off, two seated, three jammed into the tiny jump seat, heads stuck up into the breeze, Gordon in a hurry, down the autobahn at 140mph. We got there in quick time, but what a mess. A 140mph slipstream for half an hour really does ruffle the hair. As I recall we had a good time at that Embassy party and finished up spending the night in a delightful little inn on the banks of the Rhine in Bonn.

Fred Maynard, the American with the Porsche, was a character and the most un-military fellow you could imagine. There was a group of US Air Force people at Geilenkirchen who were in charge of the nuclear weapons that we were armed with, they were American and under their direct control. There were about ten US Officers on the base one of whom was Fred. He was young, single and not quite sure why he was in the US Air Force or why he was here in Europe looking after some nuclear weapons on a foreign air base. He was a bit of a nerdy type, a most likeable fellow. We took Fred on board, he was good company. His Porsche however, got him into a bit of strife on several occasions, it was a hot car, Fred was not a hot driver. One evening we were in the mess bar minus Fred when a phone call comes in, it's Fred, he's in a bit of bother in a nearby village. We race off to help, well, you had to laugh. Fred's lovely Porsche was on its side amongst a pile of hedge bushes, several not very happy elderly German men were haranguing him. It transpires that Fred had taken a corner that defeated even the Porsche's legendary road holding ability. He had lost it, spun out, and demolished a local resident's front hedge, the resident was not pleased. We had an interesting time helping Fred deal with this, an exercise in public relations, I think we did fairly well in the end. Fred paid for a new hedge to be supplied by the local nursery and the elderly German fellow, whose hedge it was, seemed to be satisfied. Fred even went back to see the chap several times and eventually got to have a beer with him. Fred's Porsche was a 911 which these days is a rather ominous number.

My TR3 was hard on parts, pieces kept wearing out, the exhaust system in particular. In Germany the roads were salted in icy conditions and this caused corrosion on the underside of cars, particularly TR3 exhaust systems. When a hole developed in the exhaust pipe the lovely exhaust note degenerated into the very loud noise of a farm tractor. One day our Squadron Commander summoned me into his office and read the riot act. 'Now look here, last night was the third time I've been woken up in the wee hours by your b----y noisy car, two things, fix it, and stop racing around late at night.' He had a point. At the time I still had a romantic interest across the border in Heerlen; on several recent occasions I had returned late, at speed, with a hole in the exhaust. On a cold crisp night I guess the sound would carry, it certainly was loud.

On the Roer river in the Eifel just south of Aachen, right on the border with Belgium, there is the beautiful old town of Monschau, real picture postcard stuff. Monschau is very old, half timbered buildings, narrow cobblestone streets, a turreted castle, slate roofs, and some seriously good restaurants. It was the eating, specifically one very good steakhouse that hung out over the stream running through the town that endeared the place to me. Driving down to Monschau in the Eiffel with a pretty girl for a big steak meal at this particular restaurant was one of life's great pleasures. The town is one out of the book, probably the most picturesque place I have come across in my travels, a place I want to go back to one day, nostalgia can be a powerful force at times. The memories are strong, it was a long time ago now, a very long time ago but I've never forgotten the place and the meals, hanging out over that stream in that old worldly setting, the timbered buildings, the atmosphere, incredible.

The TR3A with its British plates always caught the eye of the young German fellows driving their Porsches, their 911s, the sight of a British sports car, top down, pretty girl on board just sent them right off, have to race it. Always interesting, Porsche verses TR3, depended a lot on the road and in the Eifel they were mostly narrow winding roads. The TR3 had superior speed and acceleration but the solid rear axial was no match for the Porsche's vastly superior independent suspension when it came to road holding so the trick was to get in front on the straight bits and deny the Porsche any chance of passing on the windy bits. It used to infuriate the German fellows in their Porsches, they would be right on your tail through the winding bits, then I just pulled away on the straights, great fun. It happened frequently, either driving down through the Eifel or driving back after a magnificent meal in Monschau. Long weekends in the Eifel, one of the great pleasures available in that area of

Germany, and a meal, hanging out over the Roer in Monschau, to die for.

There are another couple of places I would like to mention, the Dutch towns of Valkenburg and Maastricht. They were not far from Geilenkirchen, just across the border in the southern part of Holland, we had quite a bit of fun at both places. Maastricht had an excellent restaurant, Le Champ Des Beaux Enfants where the steaks were superb, real beef, we took to having a meal there whenever we were in the area. Valkenburg's claim to fame was a hill, hills are rare in Holland, the only ones that exist are in the Valkenburg area. It also had a dance hall that we visited occasionally, not a particularly successful spot for us however, the local Dutch girls seemed to be a little bit uncomfortable in our presence, we did try though.

During the early 1960s in Europe everything Italian was 'in.' The film La Dolce Vita, starring Anita Eckberg, was popular. One evening we went to see it at a cinema in Aachen, interesting, all in Italian with German sub titles, but we got the general idea. Nightclub music was all Italian as well. One evening in a local night spot the star act was a very attractive Italian girl, who was not wearing very much, singing Italian songs and singing them extremely well. What was different and certainly caught our attention was a large snake that had wrapped itself around this girl, it was damned near making love to her as she sang, very different and very very interesting. I recall Gordon on one occasion missing his mouth with his beer while watching this performance.

Towards the end of 1960 when Harry and I had been on the Squadron for nine months I became eligible for an all expenses paid two month trip back to New Zealand. As it turned out the timing for this lengthy absence from Geilenkirchen could not have been better. The leave was part of the deal under which I had joined the RAF from New Zealand back in 1955. Off I went, very timely, I had just been acquitted at that court-martial. Mother was very pleased to see me, it had been five years. Not so impressive was her failure to recognise me as I walked across the tarmac at Whenuapai airfield in Auckland. I travelled the last part of my journey home in a TEAL Electra, this was significant. I had made up my mind that my career in the RAF would not go the full twelve year term. I would be exercising the option to leave after eight while I was still young, return to New Zealand, become a pilot with TEAL, Tasman Empire Airways Ltd, New Zealand's international airline, and fly around the Pacific for the rest of my days. All these things eventually happened however there were a few hiccups on the way. With the future in mind I arranged an interview with TEAL while I was in Auckland, I was young, New Zealand born, had a civil licence, was RAF jet trained and would be available in two and a half years time. This appeared to tick all the boxes with TEAL who were thinking about re-equipping with big jets. When I advised them that I was currently flying multi jets I just knew I was in, an applicant with multi jet experience, just the ticket. Unfortunately I did not get anything in writing, I did not ask. This turned out to be a big mistake. The apparent enthusiasm shown at my interview convinced me I had it made. At the time there were very few people in New Zealand with multi jet experience, certainly none in TEAL.

The two months in New Zealand passed quickly. Mum and I travelled around the country like tourists and had a good look at our land. I enjoyed this because I had not really seen much of my home country, I was just 19 years old when I left and had not been to many parts of New Zealand. There was no family home for us, Dad had passed away just before I left to join the RAF five years earlier and the family home had been sold. My older brother had moved to Paris and was making a name for himself in the opera world, Mum was working and boarding in Auckland. Mum and I took the opportunity to see New Zealand. It was all over quite quickly, there was a tear filled farewell as I set off back to Germany, don't worry Mum I will be back in just two and a half years to take up a position with TEAL, naive me, I did not have it in writing.

I travelled back to Europe in several different military and civilian aircraft, it took an interesting turn in Turkey. I was on a British Eagle DC6 charter flight that broke down during a stop in Istanbul, great, never been here before. I managed to spend four days in a cliff top hotel looking out over the Sea of Marmara, did all the sightseeing things, visited a lot of mosques, spent some time in the Grand Bazaar where you can buy gold, if only, took a trip in a dhow across the Bosporus to Asia and spent some time with the girls who were crewing the flight. It was a charter flight, the crew consisted of a few guys and some very attractive English girls. We were all accommodated in a rather plush hotel while the aircraft was repaired, this took some time as we had to wait for spare parts. Well here I was, an RAF jet jock amongst this lot, definitely had bragging rights!

3 Squadron

I arrived back at Geilenkirchen in February 1961 happy with the knowledge that my future was falling into place and walked straight into a brick wall, my squadron had been disbanded and all the personnel posted elsewhere. You've got to be kidding me? 59 Squadron had indeed been disbanded their role taken over by 3 Squadron. In reality the existing 59 had simply changed its name to 3. The existing 3 Squadron had been disbanded. No: 3 had been a night fighter outfit flying Javelins also based at Geilenkirchen, the night fighter squadrons were bearing the brunt of another of the RAF's downsizings. The older more famous squadron titles were being retained and distributed to existing active Squadrons. 3 Squadron had been one of the very first to be formed in the old Royal Flying Core way back in 1912 so it had been decided to keep the number alive. During my absence I had been transferred from 59 to 3. Our South African boss was gone replaced by an English chap, Wing Commander Ross. A rather short jovial fellow who we irreverently referred to as 'Fatty.' He was a good boss and I was to get on well with him. I settled back into the squadron routine and it was not long before more interesting experiences came my way. During my absence Harry had to suffer flying with all the other squadron pilots, he had also gone off back to England and married, something he had kept pretty quiet. He had moved out of the Officers Mess into a small flat in Geilenkirchen village with Gillian, his new wife. The political situation in Europe was deteriorating, the feeling was a shooting war could break out at any time. Our flying took on a serious edge and the squadron went onto a permanent fifteen-minute alert status. This meant that we had to be able to launch a nuclear armed aircraft inside fifteen minutes with the rest of the squadron following not far behind. This alert status was to be permanent, twenty-four hours, seven days. Our freedom was suddenly restricted, we now had one crew permanently suited up ready to go in a nuclear armed aircraft that was in a hardened bunker at the end of the runway. Most of the tension centred on Berlin. This was brought home to me with considerable impact during a visit to that city in 1961. Geilenkirchen fielded a rugby team, as I hailed from New Zealand it was assumed I was a competent rugby player, well yes, there was some truth to this. I was a big fan of the game and when I was younger I had been in the Marlborough College under fifteen rugby team, then the first fifteen. However, I was not the world's greatest player. Never the less I was summarily drafted into the Geilenkirchen rugby team. This turned out to be very fortuitous for a couple of reasons, one, I liked playing rugby, and two, we got to play 'away matches' at numerous military bases around Germany the prize one being RAF Gatow in the British sector of West Berlin. Playing Gatow meant travelling to Berlin for a weekend, I managed this on several occasions. One trip in particular will remain forever in my memory, the weekend of August 12th and 13th 1961. We had played Gatow on the Saturday afternoon in the old 1936 Olympic Stadium, it was a huge place that had survived the war intact, very impressive. This same stadium was the scene of numerous Nazi rallies in the 1930s, you will probably have seen pictures of it in old newsreels from that time.

On the Saturday evening of that fateful weekend there was tension in the city. Around midnight there was some activity at the Brandenburg Gate near the city centre. The East Germans were erecting a barbed wire barrier right across the western side of the Brandenburg Gate. This was the start of the infamous Berlin Wall. The next morning, Sunday, we went along to the Brandenburg Gate, which was the point where we had been allowed to cross into East Berlin. It was not a pretty sight, an ugly barbed wire barrier barred all access to the east, this was the way it was to be for the next twenty-eight years. We went back to Geilenkirchen at the end of that weekend somewhat subdued, our flying took on an even more intensive edge, there was a lot more LABS training on the Nordhorn range.

That August weekend in Berlin all those years ago was a moment in history, I was there, part of it. During the course of the rugby game on the Saturday afternoon in Hitler's old Olympic Stadium, I was carried off with cracked ribs, damn, off flying for a bit, that's it I've played my last rugby game, and it was indeed my last rugby game. Later that same day the Soviets started building the Berlin Wall. I was 25 years old.

Brandenburg Gate – August 1961

At the end of October 1961 the Soviets moved a large tank force into East Berlin, there was a tense eighteen-hour standoff between a Soviet tank force and a similar American one across the famous

Checkpoint Charlie in the American Sector. Both tank forces were commanded by a General.

Back in the Zone, as the British sector of West Germany was known, 3 Squadron went onto a high state of alert. History reveals that this incident was the closest point at which the Cold War came to being a very hot war, the Doomsday Clock came very close to midnight. If either of the opposing Generals eyeballing each other across Check Point Charlie had fired a shot then the world would be a very different place today. There was to be another similar incident the following year, the Cuban missile crisis where the world again came dangerously close to nuclear conflict.

RAF Gatow was an interesting place, its primary purpose at the time was to give the Royal Air Force a presence in the divided city. There was a substantial runway there but it was only used occasionally by light aircraft. The East German border ran along the top of a slope on one side of the airfield. The East Germans had built a sewage farm at the top of this slope right on the border, periodically they would release raw sewage that would run down the sloping ground into Gatow. When the Berlin wall was constructed initially it was a barbed wire affair, it was progressively replaced with a more substantial cinder block structure except where it ran along the Gatow perimeter, there it remained a barbed wire barrier. The wags reckoned that this was to allow the sewage a free run. Apparently the real reason was to allow easy access into Gatow for an East German tank unit stationed right next to the airfield in the event of hostilities breaking out.

Gordon Glennie came along to Berlin on a couple of occasions. Perhaps I should tell you a bit more about my two close friends, Harry and Gordon. The three of us must have appeared a slightly odd trio, we had formed a strong friendship yet we were the most diverse characters, an Englishman, a Scotsman, and a Kiwi, the sort of thing jokes are made of. Myself? Well I was a colonial lad at heart, bit rough at the edges, always out for a bit of fun and rather prone to getting into strife from time to time. Harry was the complete opposite, a polite well spoken quiet and reserved English gentleman with a great sense of humour. He had the ability to never get himself in the poo. He was a bit younger than me, fresh out of nav school, Geilenkirchen was his first squadron posting, a baptism of fire. His B(I)8 role was about the most frightening experience a navigator could be subjected to, Harry just took it all in his stride. At Geilenkirchen he developed into a very skilled operator indeed. He seldom commented on what must have been some terrifying experiences I subjected him to. Harry liked to have a beer with the boys and was a good guy to have along, there was one thing however that caused me a bit of angst from time to time, his penchant for smoked kippers, Harry liked a smoked kipper for breakfast. These things were not familiar to me in fact I don't think I had come across them before I met Harry. Kippers were certainly not on the menu in the mess at Geilenkirchen however on numerous occasions, when we were away from Geilenkirchen, Harry would manage to rustle up a smoked kipper for his breakfast. You need a strong constitution to last through a breakfast with one of those things on the breakfast table, we gave Harry considerable stick when he pulled this stunt. He did confide in me that he thoroughly enjoyed a kipper for breakfast.

Gordon, a Scotsman, was a totally different character. He embodied all those characteristics that epitomise a Scotsman, a strong accent, a penchant for single malt whisky, a healthy dislike of the English domination of his country and a huge love for life. Geilenkirchen was his first posting, he was the assistant station equipment officer but in reality I think he ran the place, he was one of those types who were just so good at whatever they did. He was tall and skinny, had a pale complexion, rather thin sandy blond hair and a strong personality.

When you live in an Officers Mess you have to pay for a lot of the services like food and drink etc, this is done in the form of a monthly mess bill. If you patronise the mess bar a little too often then the monthly mess bill can be substantial, in Gordon's case this was a common occurrence. It was not unusual for his mess bill to exceed his income, I might add that we all had this problem from time to time. I think Gordon's family in Scotland must have been fairly well off, he never commented on this however, I do know they bailed him out on numerous occasions. Then there was his car, that Daimler, let's face it, we were just plain envious, wish we had parents like that! Gordon smoked a pipe, a smelly pipe, Harry and I were non smokers. We retaliated from time to time by smoking really smelly cigars but for me this was not the brightest thing to do, although rather enjoyable, cigars did not agree with me. Whatever Gordon did he did to the limit, he was a lot of fun to have around and for a Scotsman he was quite generous as well. There was one incident that occurred during a rugby trip to Gatow, he was not a rugby player but he always involved himself in the social side. We were given a list of bars and nightspots in East Berlin that were forbidden to western servicemen; this was in the days before the wall when we were allowed into East Berlin. Well Gordon regarded this as a 'must visit' list and one night he did just that without our knowledge. The bars and nightclubs in the western sector of the city were vastly superior to what was available in the East, there was little incentive to go into East Berlin at night, however because something was forbidden Gordon could not help himself. Apparently there were several places in the East that were a bit dodgy, hence the forbidden list. If any of us had been picked up by the STASI, the East German Secret Police, and had they been able to determine just who we were, then it could have become messy. I have often wondered about just how efficient the East Germans and their Secret Police really were. When we went to Berlin to play rugby a big attraction was being able to go across into East Berlin, military personnel were allowed in. We always took advantage of this, crossing through at the Brandenburg Gate. There was a Polish culture shop not far from the gate where we used to buy Supraphone records for next to nothing, classical music only, I still have some of them. Bus tours around East Berlin were popular, they would take us to all these war memorials and cemeteries for the great Soviet liberators of 1945 and even more impressive statues of the great communist leaders of the day, these were the only places that tour buses seemed to visit. When I think about it now I have to wonder a bit. Here was me, one of NATO's nuclear strike pilots with valuable targeting information in my head, wandering around East Berlin at the height of the Cold War, John Le Carré would love it. Remember though, I was in my early 20s and bullet proof, nothing was going to happen to me.

Perhaps a note about the Berlin pubs, they were great. There were numerous beer cellars, real underground affairs where the beer was served in large steins, yes those steins are not just tourist gimmicks the Germans really do drink out of them and yes they do hold a lot of beer. We enjoyed all that Berlin had to offer every time we visited the place. One thing I thought was quite a novelty, the telephones in the nightclubs. Berlin had a lot of nightclubs, basically a place where boy can meet girl. We did not find it necessary to go to a nightclub to achieve this, the pubs were more than adequate. In the nightspots, the tables where you were seated had a telephone and a mast affair that displayed a large number. The idea was to scan the nightclub for the pretty girls then dial the number displayed at their table, different! What was different was there you were enjoying a stein and the phone would ring, German girls were not backward in coming forward, they all spoke good English too. Gordon's accent however did prove to be a bit of a mixed asset in these situations, enough about Berlin, back to the flying at Geilenkirchen.

All the low flying tended to lead to some practises that were not generally accepted as routine, one of these was a manoeuvre called a buzz and break. Normally when an aircraft returns to an airfield it joins the circuit at 1000 feet, flies a base leg, and lands, all a bit ordinary, especially when you are on an adrenalin high having just spent a couple of hours roaring around the countryside very fast, just as low as you can go. We could spice this up a bit with a buzz and break. To do this you position the aircraft downwind from the airfield then blast along the runway very low and fast. About halfway along you pull up, roll to the left, close the throttles and roll out at 1000 feet going down wind. To kill the excessive speed we opened the bomb bay doors, extended the flaps, and lowered the landing gear, all at the limit speeds for these devices and kept the throttles closed. If you got it all just right then you closed the bomb bay doors on short finals and touched down at the correct speed still without opening the throttles. This was quite a spectacular and noisy piece of flying and a lot of fun, we did advise the tower we were going to do a buzz and break, tell them, don't ask them. The buzz and break became fairly common practise for 3 Squadron, we were good at it, then came the day when it all went horribly wrong.

At Geilenkirchen we were frequently host to other NATO Squadrons who would be deployed to our airfield and operate out of Geilenkirchen for a week or two. On one of these occasions we had an RAF Javelin Squadron visiting from England. These chaps had observed our Canberras doing buzz and breaks, they must have decided that this was for them as well. The Gloster Javelin was a big twin engined delta wing all weather night fighter that operated with a crew of two, a pilot and a radar operator, they usually operated in pairs, that's two aircraft flying together. They took to doing buzz and breaks in a pair formation which was quite spectacular I must admit. One day a pair of Javelins came in fast and low, the lead aircraft pulled up, rolled to the left and just as his wingman pulled up to follow, the lead aircraft disintegrated, pieces of Javelin filled the sky and rained down all over the airfield. The second aircraft discontinued the manoeuvre and disappeared away to the right. This tragedy was witnessed by hundreds on the ground, everyone was shocked into silence. Station personnel were organized into small teams to scour the airfield for pieces of the aircraft and the remains of the two-man crew, it was not a pleasant task. What had happened? It transpired that when the lead Javelin had pulled up he had simultaneously rolled to the left which is what the Canberras had been doing all along, this places a much higher G load on the up going wing which in this case had failed and caused the rest of the aircraft to break up. When this was determined buzz and breaks were suddenly way out of favour. With time the practice gradually returned, with reservations, pull up first, then roll. It says a lot for the sheer structural strength of the B(I)8 that a similar occurrence had not befallen 3 Squadron. The B(I)8 was purpose built for low flying, it was very strong, this must have saved our skins on many occasions because we sure pulled plenty of G on those buzz and breaks.

The Javelins at Geilenkirchen did not have a very happy time, there were three resident squadrons and numerous visiting ones. Their role was the night fighter defence of the West which meant that most of their flying activity took place at night, this restricted their social life somewhat. From what we could gather they pushed the limits a bit as well, they never said much about what they got up to however, on one occasion a Javelin returned to Geilenkirchen with two shell holes in it, interesting.

Perhaps I should tell you what our low flying in Germany was like. An exercise called a 'low low' was fairly representative. It was a two hour low level flying exercise around Northern Germany the purpose being to hone our skills in this area of flying. In my case I would practise all the techniques of low flying that I had picked up and those that I had developed myself, in Harry's case, how to further improve his low-level map reading ability. We would get airborne from Geilenkirchen, fly north at around a thousand feet to the nearest designated low flying area where we would drop down to just above the ground and start the exercise. The whole of Northern Germany was covered with low flying areas. We would pre-plan the sortie to enable us to fly through a string of them without having to increase our height. The usual speed was between 250 and 300 Knots. Sometimes, when an attack on a specified target was included in the exercise, we increased the speed to 330 knots for the attack. I would be trying to stay as low as possible while maintaining a very sharp lookout for all the bad things like power pylons, cables, tall trees, church steeples, high bridges, large aerials, small hills, the list was endless. The reader may be thinking, what's the problem, it should not be too difficult to see those sorts of things. The problem was poor visibility, lack of height, and our speed. It was nearly always murky over Germany and at our speed and height these obstacles just suddenly appeared out of the murk right in front of you, an immediate response was essential. Another potentially deadly problem was other low flying aircraft, there were a lot of them using these low flying areas, however, in reality we seldom saw another aircraft, probably because of the poor visibility. I do not want to think too much about that, there was a lot of luck involved. Harry would lie prone, right up in the transparent nose cone of the aircraft, and map read from a hand held map just like you do in a motor vehicle. These days it seems incredible that there we were in the 1960s, all set to deliver a nuclear bomb onto Eastern Europe and all we had to help us was a hand held map, hard to comprehend? The reality was that we developed this technique into a remarkably effective method for doing the job. Harry's favourite ground features were rivers, streams, main roads, church spires, plenty of those in Germany, tall buildings, lines of power pylons, etc. There was constant talking between the two of us, this type of flying was very much a team effort. Harry was constantly asking me to look in such and such a direction to try and locate a particular feature, my field of view from the pilot's canopy was vastly superior to that from the aircraft's nose cone. Harry's map reading skills were incredible, it was a rare occasion when he had to admit that he was not sure where we were. When this did happen we would increase our height a little and the area of countryside that could be seen would increase dramatically, it would not take long to locate ourselves. Harry's instructions to me would go something like this; 'can you fly parallel to that road away on the right until you see a bridge, then turn onto a heading of 255, hold 255 until we cross a small stream then turn further left, about 40 degrees and look for a church steeple, it should come up dead ahead; just before the steeple turn right onto 230, hold that for about two minutes then look for a main road coming in from our rear right.' This type of navigation would go on for the whole sortie, it was quite exhausting, extreme concentration was required, the slightest relaxation could result in something frightening happening, a power pylon, a cable, a tall tree, there was no time to relax, remember we were usually doing this in poor visibility. On the positive side, I loved it, a real adrenalin rush. This method of getting around the countryside was remarkably accurate. It was unusual for us not to know exactly where we were at any given moment, but then we did a lot of it, we were both well practised in all the various skills. At the end of the exercise we would arrive back in the Geilenkirchen area, climb up to a thousand feet and join the circuit for a landing, 'no, boring, let's drop down and do a buzz and break right off the deck.'

There were other exercises as well and some of them took us into unfamiliar areas. On one occasion we went way up north over Denmark into Norway where we carried out a simulated attack deep inside a fjord from low level. This was quite an experience, bit spooky as well, we were in amongst the mountains, way outside our comfort zone.

During our time in Germany we became aware of some of the more unpleasant aspects of the Cold War. Something we were asked to keep in mind was the apparent fixation the East German authorities had for keeping files on everybody, particularly their potential adversaries, that included us. NATO pilots would be of particular interest to the East Germans and we were the ones most likely to fall into their hands. They could have plucked us of the street in East Berlin if they were serious or was it that they were just incompetent, who knows? Anyway we were advised that should we have a bad hair day and finish up with the East Germans we could expect to be confronted with details of some of the more unpleasant things that may have occurred in our lives. It was all about breaking our spirit and extracting information. The imagination runs riot, how would they ever know that Grandma's first husband, who I never met and who Grandma would never talk about, was an alcoholic and spent time in jail in far off New Zealand. Would this upset me? I don't think so! What about uncle Bob, he was a bit different, we all thought he was a closet gay, now that could be pretty devastating to be confronted with and then there was something I have only found out about in recent years. My alcoholic Grandfather, who I was not allowed to know about when I was a child, only married Grandma after my dad was born, now there was something that could be mind-blowing, I wonder if they ever discovered that? What else would they know, more to the point, how would they have found out. Apparently the East Germans placed great emphasis on sexual behaviour. Well there you go, around our squadron, given half a chance, it would have been all lust and orgy which we considered pretty normal. We were told this East German preoccupation for having files on everyone had got to the ridiculous stage. The West

German authorities were constantly picking up espionage suspects, usually West German citizens who were being blackmailed because they had relatives in the East. The spying was at a very unsophisticated level. It was probable there would be several East German informants amongst the civilians employed at Geilenkirchen. This caused us to look at the pretty young things who were waitresses in the mess in a whole new light. No more making passes at Fina when she made those cow eyes while serving the soup.

After being at Geilenkirchen for a while I noticed that occasionally a few of the pilots, and there were plenty of them, three Javelin squadrons and us, appeared to have various small nervous twitches, the tick of an eyelid, or a facial muscle. This was 'the twitch,' popular belief was that it only afflicted fighter jocks. Strike pilots were not prone to that sort of thing, yeah right! We were young fit and healthy, what we did not realize was we were operating right on the limit of the body's ability to cope with the nervous tension. Eventually there were consequences, they manifested themselves as 'the twitch.' It did not worry me, I was young and bullet proof certainly not a candidate for the twitch, but then one evening during dinner in the mess I had trouble with the soup, I could not get the soup spoon to my mouth without spilling the lot. This was rather embarrassing, I thought it was probably the aftermath of a hangover, a common occurrence at Geilenkirchen. This difficulty persisted however, then it extended to breakfasts when the spoon of cereal and milk became troublesome. I developed a two handed approach to soup spoons and wondered just what the problem could be, then one day, realization, I had the twitch, a twitchy right hand. Had Fina noticed, was this devastating fact now on my East German file? This twitch would sometimes make itself apparent while flying but usually I was so absorbed with the task in hand that it would pass unnoticed. I do recall one occasion however where I did notice and it was not my right hand. I was flying number two in a pairs operation in very poor weather, low cloud and light rain, we were low level, we were always low level and bad weather was not supposed to worry us, remember we are an all weather strike outfit. We were thundering along dodging the trees and the power pylons, I was having trouble just keeping the lead aircraft in sight when I noticed my right foot was shaking, shaking a lot actually. What's the problem? Oh s—t, the twitch! We continued the flight, about a one-hour affair on this occasion, which was physically very demanding. Eventually we returned to Geilenkirchen and that's when my twitch became quite bad. The idea was to do a pairs landing, the airfield was socked right in, I could not see much at all. The lead aircraft advised he would do an abbreviated approach utilising the ILS (instrument landing system) and that I should stick with him, so I 'stuck.' I saw the runway just before we touched down. At this point I became very aware of my right foot, it was jumping all over the place. We taxied in and I took a long time getting out, I just did not know what my foot was going to do. In the event it behaved itself and I could walk normally. What to do? what could I do? I just forgot about it, the foot thing did not re-occur, well put it this way, I never noticed it again. My spoon problem however stayed with me for the rest of my time at Geilenkirchen.

I was not aware of any real downside to having a bit of a twitch in my right hand, I did not think too much about it. The underlying nervous tension, which was probably the cause of it all could also be the reason why the mess bar did such good business. The RAF had a very casual approach to alcohol, it was freely available at Geilenkirchen, drinking sessions, and the consequent hangovers, were fairly common and not frowned upon. The drinking culture in Germany was very different to that on 24 Squadron but so was the flying. On 24 we were always off around the world, usually a small close-knit group of six or seven people, which included NCOs, there was usually a big difference in our ages. The type of flying we did was pretty safe, drinking was not a big feature of our lifestyle. In Germany it was totally different, we were all young, gung ho, and bullet proof, having a glorious time flying our hot jets 'right on the edge.' Although we did not appreciate it at the time we were all pretty strung out nervously. It was this that probably led to what was at times an excessive indulgence in alcohol, I think that's the way higher authority wanted it, a way to unwind.

Now let me tell you about our secondary role, interdiction which means attacking the enemy in the immediate area of the battlefield and disrupting his supply lines in the rear areas, in other words shooting up everything that moves on the ground, pilot's nirvana. Perhaps not for everyone but it certainly was for me, thc B(I)8 was incredibly effective in this role. Conventional guns and bombs were used for interdiction, nothing nuclear. Because of its substantial fuel load the B(I)8 was able to prolong an attack and its large size allowed it to carry a fearsome array of weaponry. Our B(I)8s could be fitted with four 20mm cannon, a substantial amount of ammunition and several 500 lb bombs. There was the capability of fitting rocket pods as well however we never got around to using rockets, there was just not enough time to do everything, remember our primary role and one that occupied most of our time was our commitment to NATO's first strike nuclear capability. A very basic fixed ring gun sight was installed and it was remarkably accurate in the air to ground gunnery and dive bombing roles. The four 20mm Hispano cannons were housed in a pack mounted in the bomb bay that gave the aircraft an ominous bulge on the underside, the ammunition was also housed in this pack and there was a lot of it. The bombs were mounted on pylons under the wings. In the gunnery role very high hit rates were achieved by the B(I)8s. When the four cannons were fired there was considerable recoil but because the

Canberra was big and heavy it was able to absorb this recoil and remain on target. A skilled pilot could achieve hit rates between 60% and 70% on a ground target. Smaller, lighter, fighter aircraft, because of the recoil, only achieved hit rates around 15%. We practised air to ground and dive-bombing at Nordhorn but because of the poor weather factor much of our interdiction training was done in Cyprus. The squadron aircraft would be reconfigured for the interdiction role and we would deploy to Akrotiri on the south coast of Cyprus where we used the Episcopi and Larnaca ranges. Interdiction was a lot of fun, especially for the pilots, not so sure about the navigators. The air to ground techniques we used were similar to those developed by the RAF's Mosquito Squadrons during the Second World War. A fast low level approach to the target which when sighted required a pull up, wing over, and a dive back down at it firing all four cannons. Four 20 millimetre canons all firing at once was absolutely devastating and with the high hit rate that was possible with the B(I)8 we were a formidable foe. The attack was broken off and the aircraft pulled up sharply at quite a low height, 150 to 200 feet. The closer you got the better the hit rate. Dive-bombing utilized a similar technique but required a steeper dive, the bomb was released a little higher, around 500 feet. It was great fun for the pilot but spare a thought for the poor navigator, he was lying prone right up in the nose looking out at the ground rapidly approaching with 20 millimetre shells impacting right in front of him, sometimes ridiculously close, then a large G load as the pilot pulled out of the dive, this G load could be severe if the pilot misjudged and got too close to the target. I found the whole process relatively easy and scored very high hit rates, all that rifle shooting at school, and those rabbits, was paying off. A few things were different when it's done from an aeroplane with two jet engines and really big guns. Close attention to lateral stability was essential, trim, synchronise the engines, and keep your feet off the rudder pedals, if you did not get these things right then you could be shooting sideways. The ammunition we used on the gunnery range was solid ball, in an actual live attack the ammunition would be a mixture of ball, incendiary, explosive, and tracer, a formidable combination. All the low flying that we so enjoyed was further enhanced by air to ground gunnery. Being a strike pilot in Germany really was the ultimate in flying.

LABS, our primary role, was different, it was the method we would use to deliver our nuclear weapon. I have already described briefly how a LABS attack was carried out, let me give you a bit more detail of just what was involved and a little of the history behind it all. LABS was a radical departure from all the techniques that had previously been used for bombing. Those readers who may have done a bit of bombing, heaven forbid, might find this interesting. The military thinking at the time is fascinating in itself. During the Second World War the RAF, and the USAF, suffered enormous losses in their high level bombing offensive against Germany, the RAF alone lost around 55,000 aircrew, much of the damage was inflicted by German fighter aircraft. The Russians suffered terribly from German bombing, they did not have an effective air defence system at the time and very few fighter aircraft. These two things did not go unnoticed. Immediately after the war there was intensive effort devoted to the development of fighter aircraft, particularly by the Russians. They came up with some very good supersonic fighters. At the time I became involved the Warsaw Pact forces had just been equipped with a particularly effective one, the MIG 21, or Fishbed, as it was code named by NATO. The West's response to this ominous threat was ingenious and dramatically different to anything that had been done in the past, it virtually eliminated the perceived advantage that the Russians had achieved with their new fighters. There would be no high flying bombers, we will go in right on the deck. This effectively removed the threat posed by the very capable Russian aircraft. A low flying aircraft is very difficult to detect and extremely difficult to attack, particularly with a supersonic jet fighter. To further press home the advantage the NATO forces had developed, these low flying aircraft would be striking at the very airfields that the Warsaw Pact fighters would be operating from. This altered the balance of power in Europe and gave NATO quite an edge. There was a downside however, delivering a nuclear weapon at ground level would mean that the aircraft doing the delivery was unlikely to survive unless there was some way where the distance between the bomb's detonation and the attacking aircraft could be greatly increased. LABS was the answer and as it turned out, a very good answer. As far as we knew the Warsaw Pact Air Forces had not developed a similar system for striking at the West but then we were not party to a lot of things. Something else that our masters were rather loath to divulge, how good was the Fishbed fighter, perhaps they did not want us worrying about things like that either.

The LABS attack. The weapon we had was enormously destructive and if we were going to survive then we needed to have plenty of distance between us and it's detonation, LABS would achieve this however the technique was inherently dangerous, this is how it worked.

An attack required a high-speed approach, at very low level, on a predetermined heading, to a 'pickle point.' This was some easily recognisable feature on the ground, preferably with a vertical dimension so it could be spotted at a distance from a low flying aeroplane. Tall buildings, bridges and particularly church spires, were very popular. Church spires were common in Eastern Europe, nearly every village had at least one. This pickle point needed to be somewhere within about five miles of the target. The exact bomb release point had to be at a specific distance from the target, the actual location of the pickle point determined the length of a timed run from the pickle point to the pull up point. Over the pickle point, which we arrived at doing 330 knots, the LABS system was activated by the pilot pulling a trigger on the control column. An interesting aside here, why was it called a pickle point? Well the

Mark 7 B28 (Mod 2) 70,000 Tons of TNT

American's who developed the system reckoned that it was so accurate you could toss a bomb into a pickle barrel. Activating the system with the trigger was called 'pickling.' It started a timed run to the pull up point. The length of this run was determined by the distance of the pickle point from the target, it was pre calculated and loaded into the LABS computer on the aircraft. There was a special LABS instrument on the pilot's flying panel consisting of two crossed needles, one vertical, and one horizontal, this instrument was activated when the pilot 'pickled.' From the pickle point the idea was to fly the aircraft so that these two needles remained neatly crossed in the centre of the instrument, this ensured you stayed on the required heading and flew level. At the end of the timed run the horizontal needle dropped, the pilot was required to immediately pull up until the horizontal needle was centred again. To achieve this a force of exactly 3.2G was required which is quite a lot at 330 kts. Keep the needles centred exactly, at around 45 degrees going up the weapon will release automatically from the aircraft and continue in a large upwards arc towards the target that is some distance up ahead. Keep pulling, keep the needles centred, continue with the loop. At the top of the loop, when you are upside down, the horizontal needle will drop. The idea here is to break your fixation on this instrument. It had been shown on several occasions that failure by the pilot to break his fixation on this LABS instrument would result in a continuation of the loop and that could have fatal consequences. When the needle drops the pilot transfers his focus to the artificial horizon. This instrument was an advanced design for the time, it did not topple. It would spin through 180 degrees as you went through the horizontal upside down at the top of the loop and give a correctly sensed representation of the real horizon again. The idea was to roll out of the loop at the top using the artificial horizon for reference, as the roll out was completed the artificial horizon would again spin through 180 degrees and correctly depict the real horizon. You would now be in a shallow dive back towards the ground going in the opposite direction to your bomb. We were required to do all this at night, in all weather and in cloud. The idea at this stage was to get down low again and put as much distance as possible between your aircraft and the nuclear blast that would surely follow and not far behind. This might all sound a bit hairy and initially it was, however, we quickly mastered the technique. It proved to be a remarkably accurate way to deliver a bomb. We used 25lbs practise bombs, we could lob these in as close as 20 to 40 yards from the target. How accurate do you have to be when you are lobbing in 70,000 tons of TNT.

The pickle point for our target was a church steeple. I have often wondered that if our Eastern Block adversaries ever got wind of just how these attacks were planned would they have gone around knocking down all the church steeples in Eastern Europe? Perhaps the STASI missed a wonderful opportunity when I had been in that Polish culture shop buying those Supraphone records.

Perhaps I should enlarge on Harry's role in a LABS attack. After he had located the pickle point, made sure I had it firmly in sight up ahead and that we were indeed on the required heading towards it, then Harry's job was over for the time being, all he had to do was hang on while I carried out the actual attack, and I do mean hang on. Harry was lying prone in the very nose of the aircraft looking out forward, he was not strapped in but lying on a long cushion holding on to two large handles on either side of the cushion. He was then subjected to a large G force as I pulled up and this must have been very unpleasant, then we would be upside down and the G load would come off, which meant in effect that Harry was now hanging on upside down, this was rapidly followed by a rolling motion as I rolled out at the top of the loop and proceeded to speed away in the opposite direction. He never said much about what he experienced up there in the nosecone but I can imagine. When Harry and I met up again at Coningsby in May 2007, shortly before his death, he mentioned that he remembered the name of the village in eastern Poland that had the same name as the military airfield that was our target. The church steeple in that village had been our pickle point. I do not recall just what that name was and I am still kicking myself for not making a note of it. I would really like to go there one day, actually see the place that we could well have obliterated with a nuclear blast all those years ago and changed the history of the world.

There was a plan B for a LABS attack, although we never actually practised it the actions required by the crew were virtually the same as for a standard attack. The downside of plan B was the separation distance between the attacking aircraft and the resulting nuclear detonation, it was reduced down to about one tenth of that for a standard attack, the attacking aircraft was unlikely to survive. Plan B was called an 'over the shoulder attack,' it went like this. Should it not be possible to locate the pickle point, or if it was not possible to hit the pickle point on the required heading, or if the pilot failed to 'pickle' at the right time, then not a problem, just continue on and fly over the intended target. The direction of the attack was no longer a factor. Select the LABS system to alternate, which meant flicking a switch, then when right over the target, in our case this meant being right over the centre of an airfield, press the pickle trigger. The horizontal needle in the LABS instrument would drop immediately and the pilot would pull up at 3.2G straight away. From this point the actions required from the pilot were the same as for a standard attack, what would be different was the point at which the LABS computer released the bomb. Release was now delayed until the aircraft had just passed through the vertical going up, it resulted in the bomb going straight up with a slight backwards trajectory, the same direction that the aircraft was now going. It was a big heavy bomb and would very quickly start coming down again hopefully dead centre on the target airfield. As you can probably see the separation distance of aircraft from bomb detonation would be very much reduced.

The old pre-war Wehrmacht artillery range at Nordhorn, north of Geilenkirchen in Lower Saxony, was used extensively by the German B(I)8 squadrons for gunnery, dive bombing, and especially LABS, there were some scary moments at Nordhorn. During my time at Geilenkirchen one fatal crash occurred there. Remember we were all very young, certainly keen, but not all that proficient in all the skills required to carry out these tasks that were quite dangerous, we were in a learning curve, it was rather steep. Come to think of it we're always in a learning curve, in fact all of life is a learning curve. Not long into our initial LABS training program I 'screwed up' at Nordhorn and it nearly cost both Harry and I our lives. We were practising LABS in poor weather. I was so preoccupied with the bad visibility and the fact that we were pulling up into cloud, that I lost concentration and failed to complete the roll out manoeuvre at the top of the loop. Realization came when the aircraft was accelerating down towards the ground again, completing the loop. Well if you start a loop at ground level, at speed, it's not possible to complete it above the ground. Poor Harry, he was looking out through the nose cone. I don't know how much G I pulled, I know I was blacked out for a bit. We levelled out ridiculously low and roared past the range hut below rooftop level. We had just completed a loop, something that in theory was just not possible and something that had already claimed lives at Nordhorn. It scared the hell out of me, we abandoned the rest of the exercise and went straight back to Geilenkirchen. From what I can gather we were not alone in suffering this frightening experience. It speaks volumes for the sheer structural strength of the B(I)8 that on this occasion we got away with pulling so much G without the aircraft breaking up. How much I pulled I don't know, I was blacked out for the really scary part. Harry did not say much at all, he must have been terrified jammed up in the nose of the aircraft perhaps realising that this could be the end of us. On the way back to Geilenkirchen I think he muttered something about 'please don't do that again.'

There were other incidents at Nordhorn, particularly during air to ground gunnery. Large canvas targets with a circle painted on them were erected on the ground, they were about eight feet high, the idea was for us to dive down on these targets firing all four guns, attempting to place plenty of holes inside the painted circle. This was rather reminiscent of my schoolboy days at Marlborough College in far off New Zealand when I spent a lot of time attempting to place bullet holes inside a target circle, here in Germany it was a bit different, these guns were seriously big, 20mm cannons, and there was a degree of danger involved. To achieve a good score it helped to get in close to the target, this meant close to the ground. Then there were ricochets, 20mm shells that bounced off the hard ground, they could, and occasionally did, hit the aircraft. The danger from ricochets increased considerably the closer you got to the ground. How close is close? Well one chap managed to actually strike the target with his aircraft on a couple of occasions and collected a couple of shell holes as well, that's pushing it.

Dive-bombing was another of our capabilities, we practised this at Nordhorn as well. Small twenty five pound flash bombs were used. The idea was to dive down on the target pointing the aircraft directly at it then release the bomb, it would continue on down and strike the target while you pulled up and away. Dive bombing did not involve getting too close to the ground. In the event of the real thing the bomb would be a rather large conventional explosive device, it would make a big bang so dropping it from too low a height could be fatal to the attacking aircraft. Dive-bombing was a bit boring, no big adrenalin rush.

With hindsight Nordhorn was a fairly sobering place, just about everyone who flew there managed to frighten themselves to some degree. In my own case it gave me plenty of food for thought about my own invincibility, I guess I did a lot of growing up at that old Wehrmacht artillery range.

All the low flying became pretty normal and we were constantly looking for ways to spice it up a bit. Before I joined the squadron one of the pilots had decided to have a close look at the Sorpe dam that had featured in the famous Dambuster raid during WW II, it was not far from Geilenkirchen. Unfortunately he misjudged it and flew into some high ground near the dam with fatal consequences. Higher authority would occasionally 'tut tut' about our low flying antics but on the other hand that was our role, we had to practise it, something we did with considerable enthusiasm.

On one occasion out in Cyprus Harry and I were low flying over the Eastern Mediterranean, we were the lead aircraft in a two-plane formation, we got down very low. Our number two reckoned our aircraft was leaving two big trails in the water from our two jet engines. Poor suffering Harry lying in the nosecone claimed that the very accurate radio altimeter which he had was reading minus five feet. Then there was the time we decided to fly under one of the Kiel Canal bridges just to the north of Hamburg. The Kiel Canal is a commercial waterway connecting the North Sea to the Baltic bypassing the Jutland Peninsula, the busiest waterway in the world. There are several very high bridges over this canal, high enough to allow large ships to pass beneath, one of these bridges was just inside a low flying area that was in that northern part of Germany. This particular bridge had attracted our attention on several occasions then one day we, or rather I, decided to fly under it. I had it lined up and was about to do the deed when at the last moment we both noticed some cables strung under the bridge. I pulled up, just, and shot across the top, geez what a mean thing to do. Apparently the German authorities in Kiel had become a bit fed up with aircraft flying under their bridge, the cables were intended to deter pilots from doing this, just not cricket. On this occasion we were lucky, but we both got a serious fright. I was in big trouble with the soup that evening.

Another antic which was a lot of fun but did not endear us to the locals, was our penchant, or perhaps I should say my penchant, to fly very low along the beaches of the East Frisian Islands on the north coast of Germany. These small sand islands form a chain just off the main coastline, it's a very popular place with beach goers during the summer months. We used to fly up to Sylt, a small island on the border between Germany and Denmark, a popular summer resort, probably because it's a nudist beach, then fly down the surf line on the seaward side of the islands all the way to the Dutch border, right down low, at speed. With hindsight, and maturity, I can now appreciate just how terrifying that must have been to all the sun lovers on those beaches, and Harry. How low is low? The official line was 250 feet, to authorize anything lower was authorising something that was too dangerous. In reality we flew just as low as we could, higher authority was well aware of this. In the real world, and our real world would be fighting a war, then of course we would be right on the deck, a matter of survival. We needed to practise the art. The downside was that it really was dangerous flying just as low as you dared. On numerous occasions we would give ourselves a huge fright that would cause us to fly a little bit higher for a while. A particular danger that existed in our area of operation was power pylons and power lines. Pylons can be quite hard to see in hazy conditions and that was most of the time in Germany. The pilot's canopy on a B(I)8 had a support strut on either side of the forward windscreen, similar to the windscreen on a car, as luck would have it when you were approaching a line of pylons, at speed, we were always travelling at speed, these two blind spots would occasionally hide a couple of pylons that were on either side of you. Well we're not going to hit the pylons, but the cables? They were just about at our flying height, we never saw them until the very last minute. The trick was to spot the pylons first. On a bad hair day you could be confronted with the decision, under or over, sorry Harry, you had about a nano second to decide. I managed to avoid being caught by the cursed power cables but there were some very close calls. One fellow came back with a couple of huge gashes in his vertical rudder, he had elected to go under. It says a lot for the inherent strength of the B(I)8 that the tail had not been torn off the aircraft with probably fatal consequences.

Quite often we participated in 'war games.' We were given a target at short notice somewhere in Europe that we were required to find and attack. To prove we had achieved this we were required to take a low-level photograph of the target. One day we were given a target in the American Zone in Southern Germany, we had to get a low-level picture of this target in the Donau river valley, it was a very murky day. Here we were flying around at low level in unfamiliar territory, which I guess, was the purpose of the exercise,

Ulm Minster Spire

when, geez Harry, that was close. We had just missed the spire on Ulm Cathedral, let me enlarge. The very old, and very historic town of Ulm is situated in the Donau river valley, its Cathedral has the highest spire in the world, 161 metres. Albert Einstein was born in Ulm. The cathedral took 500 years to construct and I guess the city fathers would like to see the cathedral survive for many more years. We could have changed history! What had happened? We were flying low over a plateau just to the north of Ulm, which is in a valley, trying to locate this target in the very murky conditions. The Cathedral spire just suddenly appeared poking up out of the murk right in front of us. We did not know the thing was even there, we had simply been given this target at short notice and told to get the pictures. Perhaps some closer study of the target area would have made us aware that there was this Cathedral spire, please do not knock it down, but this was the way war games were played in the 1960s.

How was it that we were never hauled over the coals for some of our low flying antics? Most of our flying was done in designated low flying areas that we were familiar with in Germany, however we operated all over Europe, usually at low level. I have to admit we were totally ignorant of other countries low flying restrictions, there was just not enough time to study all the relevant information, particularly in a short notice strike operation, we just did what we were trained for, go in low and fast. In the real world there would be consequences, you cannot go around terrorising the locals with fast noisy low flying jets, but we did, and we got away with it. The Belgian Air Force occasionally demonstrated just how dangerous low flying over other countries could be. The Belgians were part of 2TAF, they had a similar role to ours, they too were just not aware of the potential consequences of low flying over other countries. On several occasions we had very low flying Belgian F84F Thunderstreaks from a nearby Belgian Air Force Base, Kleine Brogel, roar right through the circuit at Geilenkirchen, the potential for disaster was enormous. Remember it was the early 1960s, the

Cold War was at its height, the threat of conflict was real. It was only fifteen years since the end of World War II. Europeans were prepared to tolerate a lot to prevent another one. The NATO Forces in Europe were pretty much an occupying power, they had enormous leeway in what they could do. If we were to be ready for war then we had darned well better practise what was required, in our case low flying. The political climate was tolerant of these sorts of military activities, a necessary evil. The locals did indeed complain about the low flying, however, in most cases it never got beyond the local police, it certainly never came down to squadron level so we were quite unaware of all the discomfort we were causing. Enough about flying, let me tell you some more about the social side.

One day Gordon Glennie suggested we seek out some of the old pubs in the local area that had a history. During the Second World War much of the Luftwaffe's fighter force had been located in this part of Germany, just about every pub laid claim to having been the favourite watering hole for the Luftwaffe's leader, Reichsmarschall Goering. Gordon did some research and came up with a list of 'must visit' pubs. We organised a day off and set out in the Daimler to do some research. Some of the pubs were certainly fascinating, there was a lot of history there. During the course of our research we consumed a lot of beer, a huge amount of beer, there were a lot of pubs, I can't really remember all the detail, I do recall it being a very enjoyable day. The locals we encountered were rather bemused by these two young Englanders seeking out Goering's favourite pubs. We got back to Geilenkirchen without coming to grief, which, when I think about it, was rather remarkable. Gordon was a practised drinker, he could hold his alcohol which was just as well because we must have been plastered. The next morning I was not well, very unwell, by midday I was seriously unwell and becoming a little concerned, a hangover, of course, but this was more than a hangover.

I bit the bullet and went along to the station doc. He listened to my account of the great exploratory pub crawl, did a couple of tests, then a smile came over his face; he advised me I had managed something that is not the easiest of things to achieve, I was suffering from alcohol poisoning. The sheer volume of beer had simply been more than my system could handle, this was the result. 'Never mind, in a day or two you will be right, and oh, by the way, you had better get down to 3 Sqdn and explain as best you can that the doc says you are not to go near an aeroplane for a couple of days.' I went along to see Gordon in his office in the Equipment Section. Gordon was well organised, he was the de-facto boss of the Equipment Section and he had a secretary. She advised me that Flying Officer Glennie was very busy that day, he had several meetings and would not be able to handle any visitors, 'perhaps tomorrow sir.' Nice one Gordon, I bet you were unable to handle very much at all. When I nailed him in the mess that evening he looked terrible, he simply said he had not enjoyed his day in the office.

During 1961 another Kiwi arrived on the squadron, Phil Pinney, a career man, just graduated from Cranwell. This was his first squadron posting; better take him under my wing, provide some guidance. This proved unnecessary, Phil was not wet behind the ears, he was right onto everything. It was nice to have another Kiwi around the place, bit of backup, Phil could certainly provide that. Between the two of us we gave the Brits quite a bit of stick. Phil came from a farming family in Canterbury, he was tall and skinny, looked a bit like Ed Hillary of Everest fame. He intended to make a full-time career in the RAF. Phil had a penchant for organising trips. During the summer of 1961 not long after he arrived on the squadron and just after I had picked up the TR3, he suggested a short trip down to Bavaria, especially in a sports car. Good one Phil, I think so too. We needed to get to Oberammergau to check on a farmhouse that took in guests, it had been recommended as a good place for winter accommodation. Oberammergau was a skiing resort. Off down the autobahn, flat out of course, to Bavaria, and Oberammergau. The farmhouse was good and we stayed for a couple of days. We were to use this farmhouse a lot in the coming months. The area around Oberammergau is picture postcard material and the village is famous for its Passion Play which is performed every ten years. The story goes that during the 1630s when the black plague was ravaging Europe the area around Oberammergau was spared the worst of the carnage, to celebrate this good luck the village vowed to stage the Passion Play every 10th year for ever. The play celebrates the life and death of Jesus. The cast of over 2000 is drawn entirely from the village. We had a look inside the theatre where the play is performed, very impressive. The surrounding countryside is covered with trees, it's very hilly with the hills rising up into mountains. There are a lot of small lakes and well-paved roads allowed good access to all the scenic places. Everything was neat and tidy, a legacy of centuries of settlement. It's certainly a very scenic area, at every bend in the road another quite spectacular panorama opened up. We had a good look around and lined up the farmhouse for future use during the winter with a view to some skiing, then off back to Geilenkirchen.

During the summer of 1962 Phil suggested a trip to Crete, bit different, problem, I'm broke, pretty normal for me. 'Not a problem, we'll do it on the cheap, won't cost much,' then Phil adds, 'oh by the way, I have these two cousins from New Zealand who want to come along, couple of girls from Christchurch.' That brought about a concentration of the mind, 'come on Phil, let's see, photos please.' He produced some pictures of two rather attractive girls, hmm, a trip to Crete eh! In the end, five of us set off for the Mediterranean, three guys and two girls. We bought ourselves some rail passes, those things that allow you to travel all over Europe by train. We set off, first stop Milan. I remember being very impressed by the size of the railway station. Not much time in Milan, back onto the train, off to Brindisi on the heel of Italy. Brindisi is a very old port city dating back to pre Christian times and not expensive. Phil had done his homework, he said it would not cost much, he had better be right, I was skint. Southern Italy is quite poor, you can live there cheaply. Brindisi has a large harbour parts of it enclosed by huge stone walls. There are numerous cheap eating places around the harbour and the setting was quite delightful. We spent a couple of days exploring the place, then off to Corfu, an island just off the west coast of Greece, in a vehicular ferry. I was keen to visit the site of one of the very early Club Mediterranees, it had been at a place called Palaiokastritsa on Corfu. We found it, a derelict collection of huts long since deserted, rather a sad sight, I could only imagine what it must have been like. I have a soft spot for Club Meds, in more recent years I have enjoyed holidaying at many of them. We found accommodation in Palaiokastritsa village and had an enjoyable couple of days there. Corfu is very pretty with a lot of magnificent old stone churches and monasteries. If opportunity ever presents itself you must spend some time on Corfu. We found another ferry that took us to Piraeus, the port for Athens, this ferry took us through the Corinth canal, a spectacular sight. We had one day in Athens eating very frugally then Pin found this local supply boat, the SS Angelica, which went to Crete. That's the one, declared Pin, cheap, cheap it was, and very nasty! The SS Angelica was seriously old, been retired from any respectable shipping company long ago, definitely the end of the line, but cheap! It was the sort of relic you might see in an old movie, the locals with their dogs, pigs, hens, cats, all the shopping, the screaming kids, no accommodation, you stayed on the deck, different! Apart from that, the trip was fascinating. We picked up and dropped off passengers, pigs, dogs, cats, whatever, as we made our way through the beautiful Aegean Islands eventually arriving at Heraklion in Crete where we disembarked. We found accommodation in a local guesthouse, again quite cheap, and retired to a local taverna where we got talking to some locals which was not the easiest thing to do. After a while it became obvious they were paying for our drinks. It got a bit embarrassing, they would not let us pay for anything. What's going on? Eventually the penny dropped, they had figured out we came from New Zealand, well four of us did, that made us very popular. It was a hangover from the Second World War, New Zealanders were number one in Crete. The next day we had a look around Heraklion then went out to Knossos an archaeological site dating back to the Bronze Age, about 2000 BC, it's just outside the town. We spent a further day in Heraklion, this time lying on a beach, then re-boarded the SS Angelica and travelled back through the beautiful Aegean Islands to Piraeus. That boat was a real test of stamina, I was a bit crook on the return trip, probably our reduced diet, no meat! We found that the cheapest meal in this part of the world was a tomato salad with plenty of olive oil, very healthy, actually very tasty, but after the umpteenth tomato salad I'm not so sure. We finally left that dreadful boat and enjoyed another day in Athens. Funds were now seriously short, the novelty of travelling on 'nothing' was starting to wear a bit thin. We caught a ferry back to Corfu, a further one to Brindisi, then a train for Germany. We pooled our funds and decided that when we got over the border into Germany we would get off the train, book into a guesthouse, and have a real meal, meat. Freiburg was the lucky town. We left the train, found a small hotel that happened to have a big bar and restaurant attached, and checked in. As I remember, it was all five in the one room, we needed the money for food. We had a glorious night, many steins of beer and some excellent steaks, real food at last. I do not remember the latter part of that evening. We travelled on to Geilenkirchen the next day, the boys back to the Officers Mess. The two girls stayed with a couple of RAF families for a few days, then went off to London. It was all over, we had been away for two weeks on the smell of an oily rag, not sure if that's the way to go but it was a lot of fun. I thought that perhaps I would not be a big fan of olive oil or tomatoes after that episode, but no, they are just fine, I really like olive oil and tomatoes.

On the subject of food dislikes here's a little story. The British Military in Europe maintained a strategic reserve of food in case of war. This large food mountain had to be constantly turned over to ensure its freshness so it was dished out to all the military establishments on a regular basis. It seemed to consist entirely of brussel sprouts and powdered potato. We were constantly being served up these small rock like brussel sprouts and tasteless potato. These days I do not like brussel sprouts, I'm sure it was this overkill when I was a young lad that did it.

The Second Tactical Air Force in Germany ran a winter survival school in Bavaria at a place called Bad Kholgrub, all aircrew were required to complete this course at some time during the term of their posting in Germany. The prelude was a week of skiing at nearby Oberammergau, a village we had already checked out. The idea of the skiing was to toughen us up before the rigours of the survival course. We were told the course was very realistic, seriously tough. Harry and I decided to do it, sounded like some good skiing. Harry could ski, however I was a novice so I thought it would be wise to improve my skills before embarking on this course. The accommodation at Oberammergau was sorted from the earlier visit so off we went in the TR3, 111mph down the autobahn, it did not take long. We did the trip to Oberammergau several times in the period leading up to the survival course and my skiing skills improved noticeably. The farmhouse where we stayed was impressive, decorated with hand carved woodwork, the sort of exquisite craftwork you see in picture postcards. Oberammergau, being such a famous village, had some of the finest carving to be found in Bavaria, our farmhouse was a particularly good example. We found out that the farmer who owned the place, our host, had played the part of Christ in the Passion Play some years earlier. This gave him considerable status, it had to be reflected in his house. The only problem staying there was communication, he spoke no English at all and our German, well it was not very good, the other thing was the smell. In Bavaria, during the winter, farm animals are housed indoors, the animal accommodation is an extension of the house the idea being to share the available warmth. Well what you had was a house, with people in it and just through the adjoining wall, a lot of cows, doing what cows do on a dirt floor, this made the whole place a bit smelly, not to worry, when in Bavaria do as the Bavarians do. We enjoyed ourselves in Oberammergau and I managed to become reasonably proficient on the skis. Harry and I did the survival course in February1962 during one of the harshest winters that Europe had experienced for some time. The lead up was a glorious week of skiing at Oberammergau, as advertised. Our accommodation in Bad Kholgrub was the Gasthof Post, a hotel the RAF had taken over, we bused to Oberammergau each day for the skiing. The week's skiing, and a bit of nightlife at Bad Kholgrub, was great, then it all turned to worms, without doubt that survival course was seriously tough. Just a couple of days into it two fellows became so exhausted that they had to be evacuated out to hospital, apparently one of them came close to death. We were taken to the very limit of human endurance in very harsh winter conditions, survival is a serious business. The idea was to impress upon us what we could be up against should we come to grief in a real war. On day one, night one actually, we were bundled into a closed truck in our flying gear, blindfolded, and driven out into the night, the very cold snowing night. At intervals the truck would stop, names would be called and those named dropped off into the snow, the very deep snow. We were not given any indication of where we were, however we did know where the truck had started from. We were handed a crude map with a rendezvous point marked on it and told to be there by 9am the following morning, oh yes, there will be a Bundeswehr Alpine unit trying to capture you, they are the bad guys, we suggest you do not get caught. If you are caught then that's it, the first part of your exercise is over. 'Hang on, this is a real survival exercise, what's this meekly giving up if caught?' We had heard stories about RAF fellows being roughed up by this Alpine unit during earlier courses, we had also heard stories about RAF fellows whacking the Germans and escaping. Made us think a bit about the state of relations between them and us. Perhaps it would be prudent not to get caught. Splosh! Harry and I are dumped into the very deep snow. 'Well Harry, you're the navigator, which way?' 'Eh, not sure.' We pooled all our skills and instincts, figured out where we were and where we had to go. With hindsight it appears we worked it out remarkably well. Off we went floundering through very deep soft snow. Progress was extremely slow and very fatiguing, we soon realised that, one, we would never make the deadline of 9am, and two, we would run out of energy long before then anyway, this deep snow was just too tough. It was a very black night, we were out in open country in deep snow leaving a very obvious trail behind, not good. What we needed was shallower snow and we needed to get away from this open ground. About this time our adversaries started firing star shells which lit up the sky enabling us to see around a bit, it also enabled the bad guys to see things as well. We spotted some high ground covered in trees away to one side apparently going in the direction we wanted. 'That's it Harry, onto the high ground and into those trees.' We struggled through the deep snow and made it into the trees. Good one, the snow was nowhere near as deep and the bad guys would not be able to see us. On we went, after a while we heard the bad guys, they were making a bit of noise. They had caught one of our fellows and were being a bit vocal about it. What do we do

Harry, stage a rescue, I don't think so, the idea is to survive. We pressed on, saw the bad guys on several occasions and had one close call. Luck was on our side, we saw them before they saw us. It was bitterly cold, our flying gear was not up to the conditions but then this is how it would be for real, better harden up. The cold and the physical exertion started to take a toll, we found ourselves having to take breaks fairly frequently. In my youth, back in New Zealand, I had been in the Scouts, I had done a fair amount of tramping and rough camping so I did have some idea of what we were up against. Harry on the other hand had been brought up in England, he had not participated in those sorts of activities, he was finding it really hard going. We struggled on and figured we were making good progress although we did not really know, we could not be sure of just where we were. Then around 8am, bingo, 'this is the rendezvous, where is everyone?' The area was deserted. 'Sure this is the place? What do you think Harry?' 'Yep, this is the spot all right, and if it's not then it's going to be, I'm shot,' 'me too, this is the place all right, I'm going to have a sleep.' We had indeed made it to the rendezvous and we dropped off to sleep.

'Hey you guys, wake up, what are you doing here?' It was one of the course instructors.

'Well we thought the general idea was to get to this place, right?'

'Well yes, but you were supposed to do the cross country trek to get here.'

'We have done the trek, dodged all the bad guys, and generally acquitted ourselves fairly well don't you think.'

'You mean you are from the truck?'

'Yep, that's right.'

'Well good show, we were not expecting anyone for another couple of hours.'

'Geez Harry aren't we just the smartest.'

It was another hour before the next survivor staggered in, that made us feel great. There was no let up, having run us down to a low physical condition the idea was to keep the pressure on for a few days to see how we responded. We were told we had four hours to construct some form of shelter and that would be our home for the next three days. Heating had to be organised which meant a fire. It was bitterly cold and that was becoming a problem. Harry and I elected to build an Indian tepee. We were given the remains of a parachute, that's the one we would have arrived in for real. Four hours later we moved into a very fine tepee, complete with fire. Food up to this point had been the survival rations carried in our flying suit, dark chocolate and barley sugar, it was just about all gone. Later that day when all the surviving survivors had arrived and constructed their shelters we were gathered together for a some instruction. 'This is a rabbit,' the instructor had a very large rabbit in his hand, 'I'm going to show you how to utilize every last bit of it.' Well he did not need to tell me, as a kid in New Zealand I had shot a lot of rabbits, I knew all there was to know about them but then life is a learning curve, it turned out this instructor knew things about rabbits I would never have dreamed about. He reduced the rabbit down to the usual fleece and body meat, I knew all about, then he got onto the bits that I did not know about. First up, 'a little warm raw liver perhaps,' ugg, then, 'an eye perhaps.' 'You have to be joking.' 'They are the most nutritious part of the animal, sure you would not like to try,' 'no thanks.' 'Well let me demonstrate.' This fellow then placed this rabbit's eye between his teeth and bit down on it, I will never forget the crunching noise. He then proceeded to show us how every last little bit of rabbit had a use, especially in a survival situation. The punch line, each small group of us were given one large Bavarian rabbit, dead, that was to be our food source for the next two days. Well Harry and I ate this rabbit which was rather good. I knew how to deal to a rabbit, not so sure about the eye and stuff.

The following couple of days were taken up with more instruction in survival techniques, improving our shelters, foraging for food, snaring small animals and the like. On the final day we were given another map with a rendezvous point marked on it and told to be there in five hours time. There would be no bad guys this time however the terrain might be a bit challenging. It was, deep snow again, extremely fatiguing, and we were not in very good condition to start with. At the rendezvous there was a pub. Hot soup and beer was laid on. It was interesting to observe what happened. Some of the fellows got right into the hot soup then threw up, others got into the beer and also threw up. The point was driven home that after four days in a survival situation you just have to ease back into normal activity slowly. After that we were loaded into trucks and taken back to Bad Kholgrub. Hot showers and bed, glorious bed, that was one tough course.

The final part was great, two more days of skiing at Oberammergau, the survival school did not want us returning to our front line units in a run down condition, we had to be up and running. There was going to be a social gathering on the final night with female company, really! One of the school's instructors, a rather handsome fellow, had established relations with a girl's finishing school that was nearby. This school was one of those institutions you find in Europe's mountains where seriously rich folk send their beautiful daughters to learn life's social graces. How about meeting some Royal Air Force Officers, that will probably be a new experience. What could we teach them? The mind reels!

Well it's the last day of skiing at Oberammergau, the social gathering is that night. I am zipping down the slopes, quite a sharp skier now, watch out, too late, whack, I ski into a pine tree, at speed. Local hospital, fractured bone in foot, plaster, crutches, bugger! I made it to the evening function, there was this group of the most gorgeous girls you could imagine and me hobbling about on crutches. Most of the girls were from Columbia in South America, extremely attractive and very closely chaperoned, fat chance guys, just think about it. A couple of days later Harry and I arrive back at Geilenkirchen, me broken, unable to fly for a month.

Graduation Diploma

At the end of the survival course there was a presentation ceremony where we each received a certificate, I still have it to this day, it reads: This Diploma is awarded to Flying Officer R C Mangin Who Successfully Survived No:3 Course which was the Coldest, Most Arduous, and by far the Most Excruciatingly Agonising Course in the History of the School. True, I had survived the course, but I had definitely failed the 'after course.'

The Middle East

In March 1962 the squadron aircraft were re-configured for the Interdiction role and detached to Akrotiri in Cyprus for a month to practise gunnery and dive-bombing at the Larnaca and Episcopi ranges on the south coast of the island. Geilenkirchen was to be closed for four months to allow major work to be carried out on the runway. When we returned from Cyprus 3 Sqdn was to be detached to Wildenrath, just up the road from Geilenkirchen, for a further three months while work on the runway at Geilenkirchen continued. This was to be an interesting time. To avoid tarmac congestion at Wildenrath, which had three resident squadrons of its own, we were to take the opportunity to do as many extended trips away from Germany as possible. I put my hand up for this, but first let me tell you about Cyprus.

Akrotiri is a large military airfield on the south coast of Cyprus in the Greek part of the island. In the 1960s it was the base for several RAF front line squadrons. There was a good air to ground gunnery range further along the coast at Larnaca and a dive bombing range at Episkopi, also nearby. Both these places enjoyed excellent weather, that's why we went there. We did a lot of air to ground at Larnaca and I was starting to get really good gunnery scores. Dive-bombing was carried out at Episkopi in pairs, that's two aircraft flying in formation, after a few sorties I started to get good results with that as well. It does not pay to be the smart arse however. One day this senior officer turns up, B(I)8 qualified, or so he said, he wanted to do some air to ground gunnery. Air to ground is not easy, it takes a while to become proficient, it's also inherently dangerous. Quite apart from the fact that you are operating very close to the ground you are firing 20mm cannons, four of them at once, there are ricochets that can be hazardous. The other worry was the low flying involved. All the pilots on 3 Sqdn were low-level specialists, how experienced in all these skills is this senior officer who wants to do some air to ground?

'Rex, you are our ace shooter, go with him and talk him through it, make sure he does not come to grief.'
S--t just what I don't need, there's only one pilot's seat in a B(I)8, I would not be in it, I would be down in the nose where Harry usually lived trying to tell this senior officer how it's done and seeing the results from very close range. Well this guy was not good, I think eventually he managed to put a couple of holes in the target but he sure caused my blood pressure to peak. It was that episode that made me appreciate just what Harry had to endure just about every time we got airborne. Fortunately soup was not on the menu at Akrotiri that evening.

The social life out in Cyprus was interesting. We knew some of the resident pilots from Bassingbourne days, these fellows took us under their wing and showed us around. It started on day one with a late evening trip into the local town, Limassol, after a lengthy session in the mess bar. Our Akrotiri mates had the town sorted. We visited a couple of local Greek bars where we were obliged to drink ouzo, have to keep in with the locals you see, not my thing but you must be seen to be making an effort. Ok, enough of the public relations, what about a beer. The local brews, Leon and Keo, not the greatest, fortunately European beers were also available. Hungry? how about our favourite 'eating place,' not restaurant, place. It was a 'café de gutter' and the food was excellent. Kebabs of all varieties were a great favourite in Cyprus, these ones came from a kerbside vendor who cooked them right there at the side of the street on a small charcoal barbeque. We sat on the kerb devouring Kebabs and plenty of beer, great meal. Kebabs in a gutter in Limassol late at night was a regular activity for the guys at Akrotiri.

While we were detached to Cyprus Harry and I did an interesting trip to Khormaksar, a big RAF airfield in Aden in Yemen. It was a two plane formation. The first leg was direct to Khartoum in the Sudan to be flown at high level. We were also instructed to go around the south west corner of Egypt on our way to Khartoum, bit strange why not just go direct it's all dessert nothing for hundreds of miles, a direct flight would shorten the trip. At the time Egypt was not a friendly country and rumour had it there were Mig fighters based at Wadi Halfa an Egyptian airbase not far from 'the corner.' It was only six years since the 1956 Suez War when Great Britain had attacked Egypt, Canberras from Akrotiri had dropped a lot of bombs on that country. The word was that you could be in trouble if you took the short cut, cutting the corner might just be pushing it, it was the longer around the corner for us that day. From Khartoum we were to fly the first part of the final leg to Khormaksar at a lower level, this would take us over Asmara a town in Eritrea on the Horn of Africa. Asmara is a big town, quite high, over 7000ft. Now, as the reader is well aware, most of our flying was done at low level, entrenched habits die hard. On this occasion we were already flying the leg at a lower altitude, as I recall we dropped even lower and flew down the main drag of Asmara low, very low, sorry folks, but it was good fun. We climbed out of there and continued on to Aden. One of our squadron pilots had a twin brother who was a Royal Navy Fleet Air Arm pilot, his aircraft carrier was visiting Aden at the time. Our squadron pal had let his twin know that we were coming the idea being to meet up for a beer. When we got to Aden we sought out the Royal Navy Officers Mess where there would be a good chance of finding this fellow. Well we had barely walked in through the door when there was our squadron mate dressed up as a naval officer, the likeness was incredible. Harry and I had a good time with those Fleet Air Arm pilots, we finished up very late trying to locate the RAF Officers Mess where we were supposed to be staying. The next day we were out and about exploring Aden, we asked a local taxi driver to take us to a good shopping area. He strongly advised us to visit an area called Crater, very good shopping he said, 'everyone goes there, I will take you, special price' and

The Author In Cyprus

Crater was where he dropped us off. The area was called Crater because this predominantly shopping area was inside an old volcanic crater. It was a very old part of Aden with a lot of fascinating old buildings dating back to medieval times. I remember buying a set of spanners, at a very good price of course, all these years later I still use them. Later that day, while we were having a beer in the mess, I recounted the story about my very good purchase to one of the resident pilots, shock, horror, 'you were in Crater?' 'yep, very good shopping, this taxi driver recommended it.' 'Don't you guys know that Crater is way off limits, two Brits have been murdered there in the past month.' 'Ah, really, ah, nobody told us.' 'Geez Harry I think we might have stuffed up.' At the time, the early 1960s, the British were having serious problems with the locals in South Yemen. There was a sizeable British force based there to deal with it. The RAF maintained a squadron of Hunter FGA9s at Aden. The FGA9 was a specialised ground attack version of the versatile Hunter jet fighter and like our B(I)8s it could carry a fearsome array of weaponry, four 30mm cannon, 60lb rockets, 500 and 1000lb bombs. This squadron saw quite a bit of action against the local tribes further inland and suffered several losses. The prevailing climate in Aden was not friendly, in fact it was quite a dangerous place but nobody had brought us up to speed on that. I have often thought about that taxi driver, was he a good guy, or were we being set up and just got lucky? The real reason for our visit to Aden was to ensure that the German based Canberra pilots would be familiar with the area should their services be required at short notice to back up the firepower of the local Hunter squadron, but again, we were not told about that either. The good folks who lived in Asmara were certainly aware of our presence however. This trip to Aden was known as a Southern Ranger, I will tell you more about Southern Rangers shortly.

While we were in Aden a couple of stories surfaced which gave us some idea of the prevailing political climate. A local Sheik had let it be known he would pay £5000 for the head of a British pilot, well it's nice to be wanted. Another story was about how to use the service 38 revolver that all pilots were issued with in Aden. I seem to recall an incident in Nicosia a few years earlier where I had indeed used my service 38, but not in the approved manner. The Aden story went like this. The drill Sergeant was instructing the squadron pilots about how to use their service 38 in the event of a bad hair day. Should you find yourself down in the desert without your aeroplane and the angry Arabs are approaching then it is recommended that you use your 38 to dispatch yourself, not a few Arabs. If captured, well there was that reward and the method of your demise would probably be flaying, that's being skinned alive something the tribal women carried out. Apparently the process could be stretched to a couple of days, not good. Now then this is how you dispatch yourself, you place the barrel of the 38 in your mouth, bite firmly, and pull the trigger. None of this putting the barrel against your temple, you will be so terrified the chances are you will not do the job properly just graze your skull and knock yourself out. When you wake up those Arab women will have you and you would not want that. 'Really Sergeant, very interesting, but about this biting on the barrel bit, not good for the teeth!' The situation in Aden continued to deteriorate, I remember reading about the final hurried evacuation of the place some years later where the Queen's yacht played a prominent part. At the end of the Akrotiri detachment we flew back to Wildenrath, Geilenkirchen was to remain closed for a further three months.

In the bar one evening I was talking to our squadron commander, 'very congested here at Wildenrath sir, perhaps you should send us off on another Southern Ranger, and is that a gin and tonic?' Well it does pay to ask, Harry and I were off to Cyprus again, with a stop at Malta on the way. 'Oh by the way you will have a Group Captain with you as far as Cyprus.' 'Ah, he's not B(I)8 qualified I hope,' memories of that frightening gunnery trip at Larnaca sprang to mind. 'No, this chap's far from current, he's a staff officer who has to get to Cyprus, he will just be a passenger.' 'Ok, that sounds better.'

Perhaps I should tell you about the seating arrangements and how we carried passengers in a B(I)8. Basically it was a two seat aeroplane, one for the pilot, one for the navigator. The navigator's seat was set low in the fuselage next to the pilot, it was used for takeoff and landing. You could not see outside from this seat. Forward of this, in the nose cone, was another small seat where the navigator could sit and operate his electronic equipment and forward of this again was a mattress that allowed him to lie prone right up in the nose of the aircraft and look out at the ground, so it was possible to fit four bodies into a B(I)8.

The Group Captain turned out to be a good sort, when we got to Akrotiri he insisted on buying us drinks in the mess bar. I stopped short of suggesting that he might like to come into Limassol with us for kebabs after all he was a senior officer. We enjoyed a couple of days in Cyprus then flew to Luqa in Malta then back to Wildenrath. During our stay at Wildenrath we got to operate to quite a few other NATO Airbases around Europe. We went up to Boda, a Norwegian Air Force Base, we got to do a flying display at a French Air Force Base at Chambley, we had a night at the big USAF base at Mildenhall in England and we did a trip to Lyneham, also in England. That trip took an unexpected turn, the aircraft caught fire while we were airborne, it went like this. We were returning to Germany when the navigator, not Harry this time, said he could smell burning, suddenly the cockpit filled with smoke. Now a fire in the air can have serious consequences, it demands prompt action. At the time we were directly over Manston, a large RAF airfield on the south coast of England. I rolled over and dived for the ground calling Manston on the emergency frequency as I went. Manston was on the ball, they heard my frantic call and gave me blanket clearance to do whatever was required to get the aircraft on the ground just as quickly as I could. We stopped on the Manston runway and received the full fire service treatment, just like the movies. It was not so bad after all. Some electrical equipment had overheated and was smouldering away producing lots of smoke, but we did not know that. We replaced the malfunctioning gear which Manston just happened to have and continued on to Wildenrath; I'll pass on soup tonight.

Because of the poor weather at Nordhorn, particularly during the winter, we frequently deployed to Idris in Libya to ensure continuity with LABS training. It was necessary to be right up to speed with LABS. The Tarhunah range was near Idris and the weather could be guaranteed. Detachments to Idris were popular. It was an old WW II Italian airfield about fifteen miles inland from Tripoli. This was in the early 1960s when King Idris ruled Libya, Gaddafi did not appear on the scene until some years later. We would fly out to Idris, spend four or five days roaring around the desert at low level delivering small practise bombs onto the Tarhunah range, enjoy some sightseeing in Tripoli, then fly back to Geilenkirchen. Idris was very hot. There was a swimming pool that I used, bad call. One day I woke up with two sore ears which became two very sore ears. I had to fly back to Geilenkirchen that day. When I woke up the following morning at Geilenkirchen I had two extremely sore ears, along to the Doc, oops, it's hospital for you my lad. I finished up in Wegberg military hospital in Germany with two seriously bad ears and complications. I had picked up an ear infection from the swimming pool that I recall was not the cleanest, this infection had taken hold and was raging. They filled me up with penicillin and kept me in bed for a few days. Then I woke up one morning with a lettuce green pillow, help? I had developed an allergy to penicillin, the bug was feeding on it, the bright green discharge revealed all. I recall a rather unpleasant week at Wegberg getting pumped full of this and that. Eventually everything came right and I was discharged. I still carry a reminder of that incident. Whenever a doctor looks into my ears, as they do from time to time during your life, usually looking at the eardrum, I tell them to come back a bit and have a look at the inner ear wall, shock, horror, what happened to you? Apparently the inner ear walls are horribly scarred. There have been no problems arising from this episode, I just have scarred ear walls and apparently an allergy to penicillin. That unpleasant incident at Idris was offset by a much nicer one a few months later. We were down in Libya again and we had a Sunday off. Several of us decided to do some sightseeing around Tripoli, might even buy a camel saddle, all good tourists buy a camel saddle in Tripoli. We were looking around some old Roman ruins on the coast just to the east of Tripoli at a place called Leptis Magna, when we noticed a group of rather attractive girls, remember we were all in our early twenties and full of confidence. We finished up having coffee with these girls, it turns out they were nurses on contract to the main hospital in Tripoli. They were a mixture of nationalities, all from Europe. I struck up a conversation with an English girl who caught my eye and managed to get her telephone number, 'you never know, we do get to come here from time to time, could give you a call.' We flew back to Geilenkirchen the next day, fat chance I had of seeing her again. Well I got lucky, part of the squadron was still deployed at Idris and a few days later the boss mentioned that he needed a pilot to transport two people to Idris, and bring two others back. We were in the mess bar at the time, 'Can I get you another gin and tonic sir, I would like to do that little task for you, it does involve a night stop of course?' Trying to phone the main civilian hospital in Tripoli from a military base in Germany was not easy, but I did manage it, eventually. 'Just thought I would fly my jet down to Tripoli tomorrow with a view to taking you out tomorrow night, how does that fit with you?' 'Ok, good, I will give you a call when I get there sometime during the afternoon.' I have often wondered what she must have thought about it all. Well I did get to Idris the following day, I did get into town on a bus, and I did take her out. We went to a restaurant along the coast and had a rather romantic dinner. I think she was a bit blown away by it all. We walked back to the hospital later in the evening, this took us past King Idris's Palace. There was a guard on the gate in a small hut and the strong smell of Turkish coffee in the air. 'Hello,' I ventured and 'hello' came back in good English, 'would you like some coffee.' 'Ah, yes, thank you.' Well it was all a bit surreal, here I was with this attractive English nurse enjoying Turkish coffee with one of the King's guards in a Palace guardhouse late at night in North Africa. Eventually I got a local taxi back to Idris, risky, and it cleaned out all my funds. The next day I flew back to Geilenkirchen. I never saw that lovely girl again, I wonder what she thought about it all?

Flying B(I)8s in the desert did present problems, particularly dealing with the heat. The Canberra cockpit did not open, access was through a door in the side of the aircraft, you had to crawl up into the cockpit. On a sunny day in the desert, they were all sunny days, the temperature in the unprotected cockpit could soar, 40+ degrees was not unusual. The cockpit temperature was not a problem in Germany but a real problem in the Middle East. Once the engines were started the self-contained air conditioning system overcame the heat, however, during the interval between getting strapped in and starting the engines, the excessive heat could be a serious problem. We had ground air conditioning units that pushed out cold air through a large tube. This tube was placed through the side door into the aircraft, it did go some way towards lowering the temperature inside. I used to grab the end of the tube and shove it into my flying suit for as long as I could until we got the engines started. The squadron's engineers got onto this problem and came up with a hood arrangement on wheels that was placed over the top of the cockpit to shield it from the sun, it worked well and several were manufactured, they became an essential piece of equipment at Idris.

During the summer of 1961 I remember being in the Geilenkirchen swimming pool one hot Sunday afternoon enjoying what you do at a swimming pool, when I spotted our Squadron Commander, 'Fatty,' arrive on the scene in an agitated state. He appeared to be muttering something, about 'where are my pilots.' This did not sound good to me, I recall spending some time underwater avoiding the boss. I did not give it another thought until Monday morning when I discovered he had managed to round up three crews and dispatched them, along with three aircraft that same evening to Kuwait to deal with a crisis, damn, bad move Rex, what had happened? The Iraqi strong man at the time, Premier Abdul Karim Kassem, had made a claim on Kuwait and had moved his army up to the Kuwait border, it looked like an invasion of Kuwait was imminent. The immediate British reaction was to dispatch part of the RAF's No:3 Squadron from Germany to stop him, yeah right. Other British forces were moved to Kuwait and a tense standoff ensued. No more 3 Squadron aircraft were sent however, we were restricted to base for a week in case war did break out. I guess the boss wanted to be able to find us at short notice should our services be required. When these chaps returned to Geilenkirchen a few weeks later they had some good tales to tell.

Had a scrap with the Iraqis developed then the 3 Squadron Canberras, which had been re-configured for the interdictor role, were going to take out the Baghdad Post Office. Apparently, in the 1960s, all Iraqi military communications were routed through the Baghdad Post Office, destroy the Post office, win the war. On the debit side was the Iraqi Air Force. They had been supplied with Hunter fighter aircraft by the British Government, their pilots had trained with the Royal Air Force, there had been a couple of them on my wings course. These fighter aircraft were just across the border, they could be a problem for the Canberras, not to worry, we will just go in low at night, the Hunters won't have a chance.

Then there was the story about the showgirls. Our fellows had been in one of Kuwait's better bars one evening when they struck up a conversation with a group of German girls. 'We're from Germany as well,' 'oh really.' It turns out that the girls were a dancing troupe that had just finished a nightclub contract in Kuwait, they were off to take up a similar contract in Baghdad. 'Oh really, we may be going to Baghdad as well, soon!' 'Oh you must come and see our show, it's very easy to find the place, it's next to the post office.' Splutter, gulp, choke, 'no, no, we've heard about that place, it's a terrible dive, you must not go there!'

Well the war never did get under way, tensions wound down, our fellows returned to Geilenkirchen, Kassem got offside with the Iraqi establishment and not long after that got himself machine gunned, his body displayed on Iraqi TV, they do that sort of thing in that part of the world. We never did hear how the German girls got on.

Geilenkirchen

When I arrived at Geilenkirchen in the spring of 1960 there was a Station Flight equipped with two Meteor 7s and a Chipmunk. This Station Flight was really just an indulgence for the numerous senior RAF officers based in the British Zone of West Germany in

Chipmunk

non-flying roles. They could keep their hand in by flying the Station Flight aircraft at Geilenkirchen. I noticed these aircraft spent a lot of time on the ground so I approached the officer in charge and inquired if I could fly his aircraft to keep them current, aircraft deteriorate if they are not flown regularly. I had flown Meteors at Strubby and had flown Chipmunks quite a bit as well, I was current on both types. A few beers in the mess bar one evening and he agreed to my request with the proviso that to enable him to authorise flights by me there would need to be a purpose for the flight. Well did this open up a Pandora's box, in effect I had these three aircraft all to myself, there did not appear to be too many Meteor qualified pilots at Geilenkirchen and the Chipmunk? jet jocks don't fly little Chipmunks. Silly them, this thing was fully aerobatic. I spent many glorious hours aerobating myself silly. There were things you could get away with in the Chipmunk that you could not do in a bigger jet, low level sightseeing in the Rhine River gorge for instance. Geilenkirchen was not far from the Rhine, in particular that very picturesque part that you see in the picture postcards with fairy-tale castles on hilltops. All of this was in the gorge between Bonn and Mainz not far from Geilenkirchen. On several occasions I flew the Chipmunk over to this area, dropped down quite low and had a good look. It was low flying which perhaps, in that area, was a bit naughty, but all we ever did was low flying, not in the Rhine River Gorge, but just about everywhere else, it was just sort of a natural thing for me to do. I don't know what the German authorities must have thought, there were never any repercussions from my low flying along the Rhine. There was one incident that could have landed me in trouble. In the Konigswinter, area just south east of Bonn, there's a castle on a hill, well there are a lot of castles on a lot of hills, this particular castle was a popular place for people to visit and have coffee. One day I was flying the Chipmunk in this area in very hazy conditions, low down of course, when this castle looms up right in front of me. I will always remember the startled looks on the faces of the coffee drinkers on the terrace as I pulled up violently to avoid the place. This whole area is home to countless old castles dating back to the middle ages, the Chipmunk was the perfect way to see it all. On another occasion a Belgian Army Officer who was based at Geilenkirchen in a liaison role was asking around for a lift to Gutersloh, 'yep, I will take you, I have the day off.' I think he was expecting a ride in a B(I)8, it was a bit of a let down to be marched out to the Chipmunk. Gutersloh was a forward fighter base quite a long way from Geilenkirchen, especially in a little Chipmunk. Navigation in the Chipmunk was done by holding a map in one hand and looking outside into the murk trying to figure out where you were, there were no navigation aids in the Chipmunk. That's ok, that's how we do it in the B(I)8 as well, but in this case we were going up close to the border and the East Germans were known to be trigger happy, would not want to get it wrong. We found Gutersloh and landed. The base was home to several squadrons of RAF Hunter jet fighters, I knew a few of the pilots. 'Rex, where the devil have you sprung from and what's that thing you're flying?' We finished up in the mess bar and had a couple of beers. I had to fly the Chipmunk back to Geilenkirchen later that day without the Belgian chap. Having a beer or two at midday was the accepted norm in the RAF at the time but with hindsight, not the brightest thing to be doing. The Officers Mess at Gutersloh was an old pre-war Luftwaffe one, the Luftwaffe certainly knew how to do things in style. The bar was a huge stone cellar affair under the main building with a grand wooden staircase up to the mess above. On a landing at the head of this impressive staircase was a big polished copper cauldron, 'what's it for?' Well the story was that if you were bounding up the stairs from the bar after too much beer and you suddenly felt unwell you could offload into this purpose built bowl, bit different, very Luftwaffe.

With two Station Flight Meteors available I was in heaven. The Meteor 7 had two seats, I flew it at every opportunity. The proviso there had to be a purpose for the flight was satisfied by me propositioning anyone I could find, 'would you like a ride in a Meteor, air experience.' It was usually irresistible however I did not get too many requests for 'seconds.' The Meteor was fully aerobatic, I spent a lot of time working up an aerobatic routine, not popular with my passengers. The requirement for a passenger dwindled away after a while and I got to do my aerobatic routine unencumbered by someone being ill in the back. It was a big shock when I returned to Geilenkirchen early in 1961 after my sojourn in New Zealand to find that along with 59 Squadron the Station Flight had also been disbanded, no more Meteor, no more Chipmunk, no more aerobatics!

One day a bunch of fellows from BAC, British Aircraft Corporation, turned up wanting to talk to 3 Sqdn pilots. These people were involved with the design and production of the TSR2, an extremely advanced aircraft that was being developed by BAC. This aircraft was going to replace the Canberra. One of its many roles would be a very advanced low level strike capability at supersonic speed. The TSR2 would exceed Mach 1 at tree top level and would do Mach 2 at higher levels. Now Mach 1 is the speed of sound, very fast, it varies a bit depending on temperature and atmospheric pressure, however for practical purposes it's about 660 knots at sea level, Mach 2 is twice that. In the early 1960s this was something quite unheard of. We were the low-level specialists, they wanted to pick our brains. Supersonic at tree top level, sure about that? we get ourselves twitched doing it at 300 knots. The actual specification for the TSR2 required it to exceed Mach 1 at 200 feet, the intention was to use it for LABS bombing which was what we were currently doing. This aircraft however would do it from 100 feet and Mach 1.15, now that's about 760kts; that would be really interesting and not very compatible with soup!

The TSR2 was an extraordinary aircraft, way ahead of its time. It was going to have forward looking terrain following radar which would input to the control system the idea being to prevent the pilot from flying into any rising ground which was coming up ahead and which the pilot could not fully appreciate at supersonic speed. That could be really handy at night. A floating crew compartment to cushion the shocks of high speed low level flight, head up instrument display to ensure that the pilot did not have to take his eyes off the ground flashing by, an ejection capsule that would allow the crew to eject at supersonic speed and many more very advanced systems. The aircraft was at an early production stage and it looked like a real goer. At the time the Soviets had absolutely no defence against a low flying supersonic aircraft. 3 Sqdn would be the first to get it. Perhaps if I extended my tour on 3 Sqdn I might get to fly one.

TSR 2

The TSR2 never entered service, it became the victim of politics. The aircraft was just so advanced, and early testing looked like all that was claimed was true. This upset the Americans who, at the time, were developing their own version of an advanced strike aircraft, the F111. It looked like the British aircraft was just so far ahead of the American equivalent that it would be perceived that the Americans had lost their leadership in advanced aircraft design. They were already hurting over the Canberra. It had proven to be such a success that many Air Forces around the world had acquired them. Even the Americans had purchased the design from the British and produced their own version called a B57. Political pressure was brought to bear on the British Government to cancel the TSR2 program. The Americans did not want a repeat of the Canberra success story. In October 1965 there was a change of Government in Britain and Labour swept into power. Labour was no friend of the RAF. The Americans put political pressure on to cancel the TSR2 programme. In April 1966 the Labour Government succumbed to the American pressure and cancelled the TSR2 programme. The whole TSR2 project became a scandal. The few aircraft that had been produced were to be destroyed, they were actually burnt, together with everything associated with the programme. The Americans wanted to ensure that development of the TSR2 could never be revived by a future Government, the new Labour Government went along with this. It would be another 25 years before the British aircraft industry produced another aircraft that even approached the capability of the TSR2, the BAC Tornado. The Americans however failed in their quest for supremacy in this area, the F111 was not a success and technically years behind the British aircraft. The TSR2 suffered the same fate that had befallen many others in England over the years, burnt at the stake! Luckily it appears that the Americans did not quite get everything they wanted, two TSR2 prototypes survived, today they can be seen at two aviation museums in England. There was even an attempt in the late 1970s to revive the TSR2 program however it came to nothing.

One day we had another NATO Squadron visit us, a Norwegian Squadron of Sabre F86Ks, they descended upon us for a two week detachment. The F86K was an all weather night fighter variant of the North American Sabre, the Norwegian Air Force had a lot of them. They spent most of their time at their base in Bodo in Norway. Occasionally they would be detached to other NATO airfields around Europe for operational experience, on this occasion Geilenkirchen was the lucky host. These fellows proceeded to let their hair down big time. In Scandinavia alcohol is frowned on, drinking is severely restricted and liquor is very expensive. I believe that at their home base, Bodo, there was no mess bar at all. Well perhaps you can imagine, suddenly these fellows are in drinkers heaven. Alcohol at Geilenkirchen was plentiful and cheap, very British. The Norwegians were a colourful lot but they were way out of their depth with the alcohol, our very British mess bar was turned into party central. We pretty much vacated the place, left the Norwegians to it, the Postwagen got all our business for a couple of weeks. I remember going into the mess for breakfast one morning and there were a couple of Norwegians, out to it, still in the bar from the night before. They settled down after a few days, I think they may have had a rocket from higher authority and we got to know them a bit. I recall taking a couple of them to the Postwagen where they quickly picked up on our finger whacking game with the chicken and chips. During their second week with us they got right into their night fighter role which effectively removed them from the bar in the evenings and we were able to cautiously return.

Once a month there was a dining in night, an institution throughout the RAF and a lot of fun. The idea was to hold a formal dinner for all the station officers, it was held in the mess and formal attire was required. Officers have a mess kit which is a military version of a formal set of tails, very smart and very expensive. If you do not have a mess kit then you may wear your dress uniform with white shirt and bow tie but really you are expected to have a full mess kit. There is an allowance available to help towards the cost and of course everyone took advantage of the allowance. A mess kit had to be tailored, this was usually done by a 'name tailor' in London. About the only time mess kit was actually required was for dining in nights and, as I have mentioned, it was expensive. My fellow officers who had career ambitions all purchased a mess kit, me, I did not have career ambitions, well not in the Air Force, so really a mess kit would be a rather expensive and short lived indulgence. I settled for the dress uniform, white shirt and bow tie option. I was entitled to claim the mess kit allowance however, then I found out that it could be used towards the purchase of a formal civilian outfit. The upshot of this was me acquiring a very smart formal dinner jacket, tailored by Moss Bros; I still have it and it still fits. The downside, it's made for English conditions, like cold, the material, although magnificent, is very heavy. Here in New Zealand, unless it is really cold and it seldom is, I just cannot wear it, far too hot, however it's certainly a very smart garment and on the rare occasion that I do get to wear it it's certainly noticed.

Back to the dining in. At Geilenkirchen we could count on about a hundred officers attending. The dining room was set up in a large U configuration, sometimes a centre table was added. An excellent five course meal with wines was served by candlelight, there were numerous toasts and speeches and the food was invariably excellent. It was always an enjoyable occasion, until it deteriorated, which it always did. Towards the end of the meal some wag would see if he could be the first to place a black circle on the ceiling and of course this became a challenge. A paper napkin was rolled into a tube and placed upright on the table, the top of the tube was set alight. As the napkin started to burn down it would lift off the table and rise towards the ceiling. If it was done just right it would reach the ceiling and leave a sooty black circle. At the end of the formal meal, when things were becoming a little unruly, we all retired to the anteroom for drinks, that's when it really deteriorated. A lot of alcohol was consumed on these occasions and it was not long before challenges between the various units were issued. There were a number of so-called games, usually involving considerable physical confrontation, one of these was called tanks. The idea was for two opposing teams to get a mess settee, the tank, from the centre of the anteroom to the oppositions end of the room. Quite a bit of damage to both furniture and people could occur on these occasions and the very smart mess kits could really take a beating. This sort of thing was not discouraged in the RAF, it was a great way to let of steam.

I remember coming into the mess for breakfast after a dining in night and there was a senior officer's Mini Minor in the anteroom. Worse still it would not fit through the double doors to the room. Apparently they had been taken off to get it in, then refitted. The things grown men do, well perhaps not quite grown men yet!

Off the coast of Germany, in that part of the North Sea known as the German Bight, there's an island called Heligoland, a German possession with a long history. At the end of the war the British occupied it, evacuated the local populace, and proceeded to use the place as a bombing range for their bigger bombs reducing it to a pile of rubble in the process. When I arrived on the scene Heligoland was back in German hands and was being rebuilt as a holiday destination and sailing centre. It was 25 miles off the coast and fair game for low flying aircraft; that was us. We used to beat the place up just about every time we were in the area. Leaving the German coastline we would get down really low over the water and roar across Heligoland, at speed, great fun but probably terrifying for the folks on the island and again, there were never any repercussions. Another place up north was Sylt, the northern most island of the East Frisian chain, a line of small sand islands just off the coast of Germany, we used to terrorize the place on occasions with our low flying. Sylt was connected to the mainland by a causeway. The RAF had an airfield there, it was an air to air gunnery school for the NATO Air Forces, all the fighter squadrons in Germany would rotate through Sylt on a regular basis. The school's Meteor aircraft would tow large fabric targets and the fighters would practise their gunnery skills by firing at these targets. There were strict rules of engagement designed to ensure that the towing aircraft survived and it was all done at altitude. The way we strike pilots saw it, very boring, much more fun shooting at something on the ground, up close and personal. There was quite a bit of rivalry between 'them and us,' the fighter pilots reckoned they were the greatest and we had to point out to them that we were the really skilled people doing the real flying.

Gunnery detachments to Sylt were incredibly popular with the fighter jocks, something to do with the place being a popular holiday spot with the younger German set, a wild night life scene and a big nudist beach. On one occasion the boss asked me to deliver a pilot from one of the Geilenkirchen Javelin squadrons to Sylt so he could rejoin his squadron there. We gave this fellow something to think about, flat out on the deck the whole way, something he probably had never experienced, he was a high level night fighter pilot. We finished the job with a fast buzz and break at Sylt. Unfortunately for us we did not get to overnight there, could not make our aircraft unserviceable, not even a little bit. I never did get to enjoy the pleasures that Sylt had to offer.

As well as LABS and Interdiction there was another activity that occupied quite a bit of our time, war games. An order from command would arrive at the squadron specifying a target that was to be attacked, it could be anywhere in Europe. The squadron was required to come up with a low level photograph of this target which would confirm that one of our aircraft had indeed found it and flown over it at low level. These tasks were fascinating, the targets could be anywhere from the most northern parts of Scandinavia to the south of France, Corsica, up into Scotland or just somewhere in Germany. It could be very close to the Cathedral at Ulm for instance. We would be given the location of the target and told to come up with the required picture within a given time frame and the time allowed was usually not long. We got to see a lot of Europe up close and personal. Frequently these tasks required landing at another NATO airfield the assumption being that Geilenkirchen had been knocked out. Harry and I got to visit a lot of airfields, Norwegian, Belgian, French, German, American and Danish NATO fields and of course all the other RAF airfields in Germany. The return trip to Geilenkirchen usually involved another strike on another target somewhere in Europe. These war games were a frequent occurrence and strived to simulate the real thing, quite often they went on for two or three days. The short notice ones that just arrived from command in the morning and required completion within a few hours, were given short code names like Delta, Amled, Tac Eval, etc. These were popular because they were usually low level strikes within our usual area of operation; then there were the Co-Ops, not so popular because these were low level night time strikes. The more serious, large scale, war games were given names like, Flashback, Lost, Gentlemen's Relish, Checkmate, Quicktrain, Backlash, and other very imaginative names that higher authority dreamt up. When I reflect on what went on during those exercises I shudder a bit, what planning we were able to do was rushed, we did not get down to any great detail, our first choice was always to go low level, that's what we were trained to do. But what about official low flying areas in these European countries? If some high level flying was required what about commercial airways, they were off limits for military aircraft? Civil airport restricted areas, also to be avoided? The reality was that these things did not get considered and I wonder sometimes just how we survived. The Ulm Cathedral episode was a bit of a reality check for both Harry and I. On another occasion we were given a target in Kent in the south of England, we had just three hours to complete the task so it was a case of strap in and go, little time for planning or thinking too much about what we might encounter en route. We figured we could do the whole thing right down on the deck. Off we went, flat out across Belgium to the channel and out across the water. The channel was really murky, poor visibility, we were fully occupied looking out for shipping, there was a lot of shipping and we were right down at mast height. Harry had calculated a heading to cross the channel that would put us in the right area when we crossed the English coast, we could then pin down our actual position with map reading, there was nothing to guide us going across the water. We both spotted it at the same moment, towering above us and right in front, the famous White Cliffs of Dover. I pulled up hard and we shot across the cliff top, just. The poor visibility had really caught us out, we were both seriously shocked, no soup tonight. Had we done some planning then perhaps we would have been aware of the 350ft vertical cliff right on our intended route but that's the way it was, jump in your warplane and go for it.

It was that incident that caused me to think a bit about how things had changed in the few short years since I had sailed up the channel in the Rangitane, had been so impressed by all the condensation trails that the high flying fighters were making overhead, the nature of warfare had changed, LABS had us right down on the deck dodging channel shipping.

Scramble: as part of NATO's preparedness for war 3 Sqdn had an on going 24 hour requirement a have a nuclear armed aircraft in the air within fifteen minutes of getting the word from command. To achieve this there was a B(I)8 fuelled up ready to go positioned in a revetment at the end of the runway all day every day. It was loaded with a nuclear bomb that only required arming to make it operational, something the American unit based at Geilenkirchen was responsible for. The two man crew who would fly this aircraft were all kitted up and housed in a self contained caravan a short distance away in a hanger, they had a van which they would drive from this caravan to the aircraft when a scramble occurred. The Americans would be arming the bomb while this happened. Into the cockpit, start up, off down the runway, and yes, we could do it within the time allowed. A crew would be rostered onto standby, as it was referred to, for a twenty-four hour period, they would eat, sleep and live, in the caravan. During a standby there was a good chance that a scramble order would arrive from command so there was no treating this rather onerous duty lightly, failure to comply within the fifteen minute requirement would have serious consequences. There was no way of knowing if a scramble was a practise or the real thing. The situation in Germany at the time meant that a scramble really could be for real, we could be off to war. Did the Americans know? did they really arm that bomb? we never knew and we could never find out, we did try. Fred Maynard, our American buddy, was plied with a lot of beer at times but he never let on, perhaps he never knew either. So at what point did the pilot directly involved in a scramble find out if it was for real, he knew the target, knew exactly where he had to go, how to get there and what he had to do, he did not know if he would survive. When he opened the throttles he would be listening for 'the word' on his radio, 'go' or 'abort,' fortunately it was always 'abort,' but we just never knew. Immediately after this initial scramble the rest of the squadron followed just as soon as possible, it did not take long. There were sufficient crews living on the base at Geilenkirchen to man just about all our B(I)8s. The aeroplanes never actually got airborne however they were all armed with nuclear weapons by the Americans, the whole exercise was very realistic. There was no difference between a practise scramble and the real thing. It was probably a bigger deal for the American unit at Geilenkirchen, they had to load all the British B(I)8s with real nuclear weapons when a scramble was called, not something to be taken lightly. Another worrying factor was the fact that if war did occur then Geilenkirchen and its stockpile of nuclear weapons could expect to be taken out very early in the piece, probably by a nuclear device.

It was a sobering realisation that our squadron was quite capable of launching widespread nuclear mayhem upon Eastern Europe inside half an hour of getting the word.

You can perhaps see although we were very young we found ourselves in a position of enormous responsibility, something we did not fully appreciate at the time but something our superiors were very aware of, the question was could we deal with this responsibility? Political allegiance was another thing that concerned our masters and inquiries were made amongst our acquaintances, the ones that our masters were able to track down, about this aspect of our lives. At times this could be a bit humorous because we were not supposed to be aware that we were being investigated. 'Ah, Rex I had this spook seek me out the other day, he wanted to know what your political views were? about all I could tell him was that as far as I was aware you seemed to be an active member of the Good Time Party, politics was not exactly a big deal in your life.' 'Any left leaning tendencies?' 'Ah, well, sometimes late at night in the bar he can take on a bit of a lean, have not noticed any particular bias to the left.' Communism was the worry, we were on the front line in the fight against it, beware the red under the bed! One thing that did concern me though, I hope they will not think I'm holding a grudge over that Court Martial but when you think that one through if anyone was holding a grudge it would be my masters. I was the young upstart who took them on and won. I often wonder if the spooks ever got to track down any of our female friends and if they did, oh dear, what would they have said?

The type of flying we were enjoying so much did have a downside. As you have probably deduced we were exposed to considerable risk on a regular basis, it was inevitable the grim reaper would eventually come calling. We were practising for a real war, the practise had to reflect what could be a reality, an attrition rate had to be accepted as part of what we were doing. I have mentioned frequently that we were all young and bullet proof, these thoughts did not cross our minds. Not long before I arrived at Geilenkirchen 59 Squadron lost a crew in a fatal crash near the Sorpe dam not far from Geilenkirchen. I have already made reference to this. It was assumed the crew had been having a look at the dam which had been one of three targeted in Operation Chastise that famous dam buster raid by 617 Squadron in 1943. The B(I)8 from Geilenkirchen had flown into a hillside. During my tenure at Geilenkirchen 3 Squadron also lost a crew in a fatal crash.

One of the exercises we did occasionally was called a high low high. This involved climbing to altitude, going to a target, descending to low level, carrying out an attack, climbing back to altitude, and returning to Geilenkirchen, not a popular exercise, we did not like high level flying especially at night. This high low high profile allowed us to strike at targets a long way from Geilenkirchen, the aircraft's range was increased considerably by flying at altitude, so was the aircraft's vulnerability to enemy fire. As I have related earlier our own war target required such a profile and it had caused both Harry and myself considerable angst before we came up with our innovative Bornholm solution. These high low highs invariably involved some night flying and it was one of these that brought about the demise of two of our squadron colleagues.

November 21st 1961. It was a night high low high on a target in Scotland, a long way from Geilenkirchen. The pilot of this ill-fated flight had approached me shortly before he took off and borrowed my torch. At night we carried a torch as a precaution against cockpit lighting failure, if all else failed you could switch on your torch and there would be light, pretty simple. This fellow had misplaced his torch and I lent him my large rubber coated one. The next morning we learnt that the aircraft had crashed into a canal near Tiverton in Devon, no survivors. The subsequent inquiry determined that the aircraft had suffered an engine failure, had spiralled down from altitude and crashed into the Grand Western Canal near Tiverton. I guess my torch is still in that canal somewhere.

During the period after I left Geilenkirchen until the B(I)8s were retired from service in 1972, the three German based strike squadrons lost another seven aircraft in fatal crashes and sadly several of these were from 3 Squadron.

The flying, and our life style, did push the physical limits at times, most of the time actually, it was a definite advantage to be fit. I realised this early in the piece and strived to maintain a good standard of fitness. The rugby helped, but a bit more than that was required. There was a well equipped gym at Geilenkirchen, I took full advantage of it and right outside my quarters was the station squash court, every RAF Station had one. I was not the greatest squash player in fact I was rather a poor player of all those sports that required hand, eye, ball, coordination, ok on the trigger finger eye thing though. This squash court was not used very much. Because it was right next to my quarters I took to hopping in there by myself and thrashing a squash ball around just as hard as I could go. Occasionally I would play a game with a mate however, as I mentioned, I was not the greatest ball player and who likes being second. Another activity I indulged in was running the perimeter fence. Geilenkirchen covered a large area that was enclosed by a high wire fence, bit like a prison I guess but a very nice one. There was a track the whole way around just inside the fence. Once around this track, just as fast as you could go, really got you panting, it was exhilarating, I did it frequently. I have always tried to keep reasonably fit and it's paid off, I'm still the same weight I was at Geilenkirchen and no health problems so far, touch wood. Bit accident prone though, broken back, shoulder reconstruction, concussion, major flesh wounds, things like that seem to have happened over the years but I class these as mechanical, not health related, how does that sound?

Bailing out; I never have. The B(I)8 pilot was a little more fortunate than his navigator, he sat in an ejection seat which had a low level capability. It was the only ejection seat fitted in the aircraft. The navigator made do with a conventional parachute. A limiting factor for the navigator was that although he had free reign to move about in the nose of the aircraft it was not the easiest thing to do. He had the prone position in the nose cone where he could lie down, look out, and be terrified, a small desk with a fold out seat just aft of the nose position where all the specialised navigation gear was located, and a bucket seat aft of this again where he sat during takeoff and landing. His forward seat was utilised when we wanted to carry a third person with us. To enable greater ease of movement the navigator's parachute was a clip-on affair that he removed and hung on a rack on the side of his nose compartment. In the event of a bad day and it became necessary to leave the aircraft, the idea was for the pilot to convert all the available aircraft speed to altitude by pulling up and climbing as high as he could, while this was happening the navigator would remove his parachute from its mounting, clip it on and wait for the pilot to give him the word. When the aircraft reached its highest point the pilot would give the word, the navigator would jettison the side door, roll out through the hole, and pull the ripcord. When this was done the pilot would eject. Sound a bit much? well the system worked, two crews successfully bailed out of B(I)8s in Germany over the years.

I must tell you an amusing tale involving Geilenkirchen that occurred some years before I arrived. One day, back on 24 Squadron, I was talking to a fellow pilot about an incident at Geilenkirchen involving him. Long before I arrived on the scene Geilenkirchen was home for several RAF Squadrons of F86 Sabre jet fighters of Korean War fame. The pilot who related this tale had been on one of those squadrons. One day fate decided to give him a hard time. He was taking off in his Sabre when the engine failed. This is a bad thing to have happen during a takeoff, it can have catastrophic consequences. He put his Sabre back on the ground, shot off the end of the runway and proceeded to slide along at considerable speed. The border with Holland is quite close to the end of the Geilenkirchen runway and this fellow slid right across it showering scrub and dirt everywhere. As he told the story, the aircraft came to a shuddering stop in a smoldering heap and he was not in the best shape. The first thing he recalls is a large fellow in uniform trying to help him get out of the cockpit and away from the aircraft. This chap turns out to be a Dutch policeman who happened to be close by when all this happened. His consoling words to our pilot were, 'Sir you do realise that you have just crossed the border into Holland, I trust you have your passport with you.'

Another incident that occurred at Geilenkirchen some time before I arrived when the airfield had been closed for some earthwork. It involved a German Air Force aerobatic team from nearby Noervenich, a German Air Force base. This aerobatic team took the opportunity to utilize the closed airfield to practise their display. The idea was to try and concentrate the display within the confines of the airfield so the viewing public could get a good look at the show. Most Air Forces around the world liked to have an aerobatic team to impress the general public, at that time the GAF did not have one so there was some catching up to do. The GAF had been equipped with the American F104 which was a jet fighter made by the Lockheed Aircraft Company, it was a 'hot' jet fighter, how the GAF came to have it is a tale in itself. During the 1950s Lockheed developed and produced the F104. It was a very high performance fighter. It went into service with the USAF however it did not last long, it proved to be quite a handful and started to accrue a bad accident record, it was soon phased out of service. About the same time the German Government ordered a large number of F104s for the GAF amidst widespread rumours of political bribery. The aircraft went into service and quickly earned the name 'the widow maker.' Well one day the local GAF aerobatic team of F104s was practising its display over the closed Geilenkirchen runway when it came to grief in a rather spectacular way. When flying formation there's a lead aircraft and the rest follow him closely, very closely. The lead aircraft makes all the decisions, the rest of the team rely on his skill and good judgment, they stick to him like glue. Well on this occasion the lead man had a bad day. As the story goes, he got into a rather untenable position at a fairly low altitude. The display to that point had not been good, rather ragged, not well executed. Off the end of the Geilenkirchen runway, just across the Dutch border, there's a large opencast coalmine. Well this aerobatic team got into a steep dive at a low level right above this coalmine, it became apparent that they were not going to be able to pull up in time. They went straight in, four F104s and four pilots. Perhaps if Geilenkirchen had not been closed at the time then this tragedy would not have occurred, who knows.

Perhaps I should enlarge on our overall military role at Geilenkirchen. Our primary task, part of NATO's nuclear deterrent, our secondary role, interdiction, both for NATO and for any requirement that the British Government might have from time to time. Most British Government requirements were interdiction missions, the Kuwait incident was one example of this. The change of aircraft configuration could be carried out in just an hour or so which was another feature that made the B(I)8 Canberra such a versatile aircraft, it certainly presented the pilots who flew them with some great flying opportunities. There was one occasion when the B(I)8s were called upon to demonstrate British power abroad. In 1959 the colony of British Honduras, now known as Belize, in the Caribbean, was under threat from neighbouring Guatemala. In a show of solidarity with the people of the colony Princess Margaret flew to British Honduras escorted by two armed B(I)8 Canberras from 59 Squadron, the forerunner of 3 Squadron. They remained there for a few days showing the flag and demonstrating to anyone who may have been interested that the Queen could deploy considerable firepower over long distances at short notice. This same philosophy was the real reason why Harry and I had enjoyed a couple of Southern Ranger flights, we were going to enjoy more of them in the future.

During 1962 I became eligible for promotion. Up to that time I had held the rank of Flying Officer, now that I had completed the required number of years I was eligible for promotion to Flight Lieutenant. To achieve this promotion exams had to be successfully completed, not a particularly easy task and you had to be considered a suitable person to hold the new rank. Hmm, that court martial, I guess they will know who I am. There was one huge incentive for promotion, Flight Lieutenants were paid more money than Flying Officers. Well let's go for it and do the thing properly. I had noticed over the years there were two types of candidate for promotion, those who got stuck in, studied hard, and passed the exams first time and the others who did not get stuck in, did a bit of last minute cramming and invariably failed. Right, into it, I definitely need the money, a change of rank would be nice too. The syllabus for these exams was wide ranging and included a multitude of subjects. There was no way a candidate could cover the lot however within the various areas that you were required to be knowledgeable about the questions were usually multi choice. This allowed you to study just a limited number of topics in depth. A good knowledge of the principles of war was required, this was a mandatory requirement. A reasonably detailed knowledge of a couple of military campaigns was also required. I loaded up with all the relevant books I could find in the station library and got right into it. One of the campaigns I focused on for a bit of in-depth study was the Luftwaffe's last-ditch attack on the Allied airfields in Belgium, Holland and France on New Year's Day 1945, Operation Bodenplatte. It was the last major offensive of the war by the Luftwaffe and a total disaster. What made this subject so interesting was that the airfields the Luftwaffe used to launch this attack were all in the Geilenkirchen area. Perhaps Gordon and I could do a little more field study in some of the local pubs. When exam time came around my luck was in, one of the multi choice questions focused on this very campaign, I was able to write up a storm. I passed all the exams first time, applied for promotion and waited nervously for something to happen. Was that court martial going to trip me up or as Daddy Drake had said, Rex they will certainly know who you are. I guess I was fortunate, my promotion came through, I was now a Flight Lieutenant.

For me Germany was a fascinating place and this fascination has strengthened over the years. I have read extensively about the country, very talented people but history has dealt them a bad hand from time to time. There is a family connection as well, quite apart from the fact that I married a girl who was born in Berlin during the war, I will tell you about that shortly, the Mangin family tree also has a Berlin connection. We are descended from Huguenots, French Protestants; the Mangins are originally from the Metz area of France. During the French Reformation in the mid 1500s, Huguenots were savagely persecuted and murdered and there was a mass exodus of

Huguenots out of France. It was an incident known as The Meaux 14 where Itienne Mangin was brutally executed that caused some of the Mangins to move to Berlin. They formed part of a large French speaking community that thrived in that city during the 1700s. From Berlin there was a move to Ireland, then some of them came to New Zealand and settled around Methven, a small farming town near Christchurch. There are still plenty of Mangins in the Methven area to this day.

Africa

In June 1962 Harry and I were given an Extended Southern Ranger to Salisbury in Southern Rhodesia, we were off to Africa. I asked the boss if we could take Gordon Glennie along and he ok'd it. We had been good friends for a couple of years now and Gordon was excellent company. We took off late in the afternoon on June 12th 1962 and headed for El Adem, a desert strip of World War II vintage near Tobruk in Libya not far from the Egyptian border, about four hours flying time from Geilenkirchen. I was familiar with El Adem from my 24 Squadron days. Flying long distance at altitude into the night was not the norm for us, in fact anything above about a thousand feet made me a bit uneasy. The weather deteriorated over the Mediterranean and we were above cloud for the later part of the flight that carried on into the night. It was not our lucky day. As night descended we encountered trouble with our VHF, very high frequency radio, the standard military communication device, we finished up unable to talk to anyone, Harry advised that his Doppler navigation system that we used for high level navigation was giving him a hard time and he could not say with any certainty just where we were. Not a good scene, night time, above cloud, somewhere over the North African coast, out of radio contact, uncertain of position and getting towards the end of our fuel supply. We carried on utilizing DR, dead reckoning techniques hoping our luck would improve. 'It's all right Gordon we can handle this.' About this time we started to think about plan B. Letting down through cloud when uncertain of position is a no no at the best of times, doing it at night over an unfamiliar coastline, well we think we are over the coastline, is a very definite no no. What are the options? Running out of fuel at night above cloud is not a good idea either. Turning north for a while so that we are out over the sea, or we hope we are, and attempting to let down below the cloud, is very high risk. If all else failed and we ran out of fuel we would have to abandon the aircraft, that meant bailing out. These unpleasant options certainly concentrate the mind. I was maintaining an intense lookout in the desperate hope that something would present itself, and it did, a hole appeared in the cloud below, visible in the hole were some runway lights. A very rapid spiral descent followed, it was El Adem.

This hole in the cloud phenomenon has resurfaced in my mind frequently over the years, I sometimes dream about it, right up there with the Karachi inspired 'toilet dream,' was it luck? fate? what if the hole had not presented itself?

There was an RAF maintenance unit at El Adem, they were able to fix our radio and navigation systems. Next morning we set out for Khartoum in the Sudan just over three hours away. More bad luck, a hydraulic problem with the undercarriage retraction system caused us to return to El Adem, problem fixed we took off again. It was going to be a long day, three hours plus to Khartoum and a further three hours to Embakasi, our destination airfield just outside Nairobi in Kenya. We have to go around the corner of Egypt remember; we cut the corner, the Egyptians will never know. At Khartoum we refuelled with the assistance of the local RAF representative, a hard case Arab and continued on to Embakasi arriving in darkness. We spent the night in the Air Force Officers Mess and took off the following morning for Kentucky Field near Salisbury in Southern Rhodesia less than three hours away.

Salisbury was a beautiful place in the early 1960s, very prosperous and under the firm control of Prime Minister Ian Smith. There were minor problems from time to time and a couple of local stirrers, Robert Mugabe and Josua Nkomo, were becoming a problem. The idea of an RAF strike Canberra visiting Rhodesia was twofold, first it would demonstrate to the locals just how quickly the British Government could deploy considerable fire power to the area to support the local government in the event of trouble, and secondly, to give the people who would be doing the shooting, that would be us, familiarity with African conditions. Nobody told us back in Germany that that was the real reason for the trip, we found out from the Rhodesians. It did not concern us too much, we were gung ho and bullet proof, certainly enjoying doing Her Majesty's bidding which was the way I think her government wanted it to be. At the time that part of Africa was made up of a federation of three states, Northern Rhodesia, Southern Rhodesia and Nyasaland, all under the protective umbrella of the British Government. A couple of years after our visit the Rhodesian situation took a nasty turn when Ian Smith declared independence for Southern Rhodesia and the federation broke up. Nyasaland became Malawi and Northern Rhodesia became Zambia. There was a change of Government in England around that time and the new British Prime Minister, Harold Wilson, deployed some RAF squadrons to Zambia for possible use against the Southern Rhodesian Air Force of then Prime Minister Ian Smith. This potential employment of the RAF against Rhodesia became a very explosive issue. The Squadrons involved were Javelin all weather fighter squadrons, the crews all British. Zambia, the old Northern Rhodesia, borders Southern Rhodesia, the idea was for the RAF squadrons to neutralize the Rhodesian air force if trouble erupted. The white people in Rhodesia were kith and kin to the people manning the RAF squadrons and the word was that if push came to shove, then no way would the RAF people deployed to Zambia take up arms against Rhodesia. It never came to the crunch and the RAF squadrons were soon withdrawn, however it was the end of Rhodesia as it had been. History tells a sorry tale of what has subsequently happened in Zimbabwe as the country is now known.

The Rhodesians looked after us really well in Salisbury. We were shown around some tobacco farms and factories, ate extremely well, and were able to purchase some copper beer tankards. Northern Rhodesia was the copper mining capital of the world at the time, it produced very good quality copperware, that's where the tankards originated. They were lined with silver and the quality was excellent, we had to see if they 'worked.' The local brew was Lion, a good drop, we proceeded to check it out using our new tankards. We were also introduced to piri piri, a spicy Portuguese way of preparing food, very popular in Salisbury. Diamonds were a big deal in Rhodesia; if you knew what you were doing it was possible to make an excellent diamond purchase. We did not know anything about diamonds and RAF Officers had very little cash anyway, no diamonds! We only had a couple of days in Rhodesia on this occasion but it made a lasting impression on me. I was to make a similar trip back to Salisbury a few months later but that was unbeknown to me at the time.

We departed early one morning on our way back to Germany arriving at Embakasi airfield near Nairobi around midday. We had that day and the following one off, we used the time to explore Nairobi. Again we were well looked after and again the eating was very good. I remember going to a steak house on the outskirts of Nairobi, the name escapes me, which was renowned for its huge steaks. If you were able to eat a whole steak then they gave you another one for free, yeah right, no way were you going to finish one of those, they were huge, and superb. Gordon did finish his but he was finished as well at the end of it. Kenya was another place that was a sheer delight in the early 1960s, now, unfortunately, no more. I wonder what ever happened to that steak house? From Nairobi, away to the southeast, you can see the very distinct outline of Mt Kilimanjaro right on the border with Tanganyika. Mt Kilimanjaro is a volcano located just three degrees south of the equator, at twenty thousand feet it's the highest point in Africa. It has a permanent snow cap and a warm crater lake. When we left Embakasi to fly to Khartoum in the Sudan, we asked the controller in Nairobi if it was ok for us to go and have a look at the top of Kilimanjaro. He had no objections so off we went. Flying out of East Africa was almost a surreal experience. Nairobi, and its airfield Embakasi, is five thousand feet high, the big blue crystal clear sky was something to behold, so very far removed from the murky conditions over Europe that was our usual haunt. The vastness of Africa unfolded beneath us stretching to the horizon in all directions, the only sign of man the occasional straight line on the surface, it was an impressive sight. I was beginning to understand why people are captivated by the place, there's an indefinable something about Africa that just draws you to it. We climbed up to twenty thousand feet and flew over to Kilimanjaro on the border with Tanganyika, which is now called Tanzania, and dropped down into the crater. It was wide, not very deep, and presented no problems. We flew across the crater lake and took some photographs with the reconnaissance camera mounted in the nose of the aircraft, spectacular, then we climbed out of there and set course for Khartoum. As we flew north the vast African countryside beneath us slowly changed character becoming more arid as we moved north until nearing Khartoum it was nearly all desert. Khartoum is where the two branches of the Nile River merge, from the air it presents an unusual sight, the distinctly coloured Blue Nile runs into the White Nile and continues on as the Nile, all the colour just disappears. At Khartoum we refuelled, again with the assistance of the hard case Arab, then took off for Akrotiri in Cyprus, around the corner this time. We spent a night there, a quick trip into Limasol for gutter kebabs, then off to Luqa in Malta, refuel, and on to Geilenkirchen, our trip to Africa was over, well not quite. Four weeks later Gordon, Harry, and myself did another trip, this time back to Luqa. We seemed to be enjoying more than our share of Southern Rangers. I was not complaining and I wondered if my buying our Squadron Commander a few gin and tonics in the mess bar from time to time had anything to do with it.

Off to Luqa. We got airborne, had another hydraulic problem, returned to Geilenkirchen, fixed the problem, got airborne again, and flew to Luqa arriving at night. We enjoyed a couple of days exploring all that Valletta, the capital of Malta, had to offer. Prawns piri piri were on the menu in Valletta, we were right into them, Salisbury had introduced us to a very fine dish indeed. Malta is quite a small island, at the eastern end there is a swimming club built into the rocky foreshore, we went out there and spent an enjoyable day swimming in the sea off the rocks, drinking in the club bar, and eating prawns piri piri. It was while we were in the restaurant that I heard a familiar voice call out my name 'Rex,' it was Peter Dwyer. The last time I had seen Peter was at Swinderby five years before. He was on a high level Canberra bomber squadron that was passing through Malta, they had a day off. A bunch of them had heard about the swimming club. Well that set the tone for the rest of the day, far too much beer and plenty of tall tales. I never found out what the strategic reason was for our trip to Malta, I was starting to look for the real reasons why we were doing the things that we did, perhaps that's why all the front line people in the services seem to be so young, you did as you were told, did not ask questions and in our case, thoroughly enjoyed it. Once you get a few years under the belt you might start questioning things and that would not necessarily be a good thing.

When we finally settled back in Germany after our southern jaunts, we decided to get three of the copper tankards we had picked up in Rhodesia engraved. The African trip had been so memorable, we really did have to have a lasting souvenir. We gave the job to the local jeweller in Geilenkirchen village. He was an elderly fellow, I got the impression he did not like Englanders, he did not do a very good job. The Os were inscribed as Ds and the general standard was

not very good at all, however, it does make the tankards rather unique. The three of them are now, hopefully, still in the possession of the families of the three of us and sadly I think I am the only survivor. Some years ago I tried unsuccessfully to make contact with

Gordon Glennie, I did hear a rumour that he had passed away but I have not been able to confirm it either way.

On that trip to Rhodesia we experienced something on the flight south from Nairobi that, with hindsight, could be of some significance. Central Africa in the early 1960s was not blessed with very many navigation facilities for aviation. We were equipped with our own self contained state of the art systems for high level navigation, but no matter what system you used it's good practise to confirm the aircraft's actual position independently from time to time to ensure that your own systems are in fact telling the truth. Getting a radio bearing from wherever you can gives a line of position, if this can be combined with another bearing from a different source then you can determine the aircraft's actual position. Radio bearings are usually obtained using a radio compass, which is an instrument that will point a needle at a radio station. Unfortunately the B(I)8 did not have a radio compass, we had to rely on a different technique to get a radio bearing. Most air traffic control centres have their own version of a radio compass. If an aircraft makes a radio transmission then the ATC centre can respond with a bearing of the aircraft from that centre. During our journey over Central Africa we called for a bearing from Ndola in Northern Rhodesia. After several requests they came up with a bearing that caused us some grief. It indicated that we were many miles from where we reckoned we were. We had considerable confidence in our own navigation systems, in fact they were remarkably accurate. We requested another bearing from Ndola. After a bit of apparent confusion by them they came up with another very different bearing that again we just could not believe. We figured that the controller at Ndola was giving radio bearings that were 180 degrees in error. We disregarded these bearings and continued on our way eventually arriving at Salisbury spot on. During a second trip from Germany to

Rhodesia, some months later, we experienced another similar incident. This happened in June 1962. Now those of you who are of a historical bent may recall the following incident which I think could be connected to our experience. In September, 1961, Dag Hammarskjold, the United Nations Secretary General, was killed in an air crash near Ndola. He was flying to Ndola at night in a United Nations DC-6B, it crashed into the bush in mysterious circumstances. The reasons for the crash have never been satisfactorily explained. His presence in Africa was to try and mediate in a local war in breakaway Katanga province in the Belgian Congo. At the time the Katangan forces employed a mercenary pilot, a Belgian, called Major Delon, who flew an armed Fouga Magister. There has been much speculation that the DC-6 was shot down. Other theories suggest navigation problems. It was night time and the DC-6 would have been using radio bearings. After our experience with radio bearings in the area I subscribe to the nav error theory.

Six months after our African trip another opportunity came up. One of the squadron pilots, Tom Stonor, had taken himself off to Salisbury to get engaged to a Rhodesian girl. Before he left he had laid it on the Squadron Commander that if a 3 Sqdn Canberra should just happen to be in Central Africa in a couple of weeks time then he would very much like to be picked up. Tom was a pal of mine and rather surprisingly there was an Extended Southern Ranger flight scheduled at about that time. I put my hand up, 'I will salvage Tom sir, he's a good mate of mine and is that another gin and tonic sir, perhaps a double.' I was in luck, the boss agreed. Harry was down with a cold so I took along Tom Stonor's navigator, Harry Broadhurst, just the two of us, we needed the third seat for Tom. This could well be my swansong, my time with 3 Sqdn was nearing the end, in fact my career in the Royal Air Force was drawing to a close, I was about to leave the RAF and return to New Zealand. We set off from Geilenkirchen on January 16th 1963 heading for El Adem again, it was late afternoon in the depths of winter, ice and freezing temperatures, this flight would go on into the night. We did not want any repeat of the difficulties experienced on that first trip to Africa. This time the flight went as planned, we spent the night at El Adem and the following day flew to Khartoum, around the corner this time, then on to Nairobi where we stopped for the night. Day three we flew to Salisbury where we spent three very enjoyable days as guests of the Rhodesian Air Force. We collected Tom and took off for Nairobi. At this point fate stepped in and decided to make our lives a lot more interesting. The weather over Nairobi packed up, huge thunderstorms, not good. Several years before I had been on the crew of a Hastings transport plane in this part of the world and amongst the places I had visited was Entebbe in Uganda, not far from Nairobi, it was a good airfield and I was familiar with it, 'Ok, we are diverting to Entebbe.' It was the early 1960s, well before Uganda descended into terror under Idi Amin. Entebbe is five thousand feet up on the shores of Lake Victoria right on the equator, it's one of the world's loveliest places. The RAF was represented at Entebbe by a very young East African Airways engineer. East African Airways contracted to BOAC who contracted to the RAF. The keen young ground engineer had never seen a Canberra before. He decided that he would need to get somebody over from Nairobi to turn the aircraft around as he was not qualified. We were actually qualified to do this ourselves, which is what we did when we operated outside our usual area. We 'sort of' disclosed this fact to this keen young chap and he 'sort of' believed us, however, we were in no hurry to get going. A couple of hours on the ground at Entebbe and eventually the weather over Nairobi cleared. We turned the aircraft around ourselves, much to the relief of our keen young ground engineer, however when it came to starting the engines, a problem, we had a starting problem with one of the engine's cartridge starters. This was a fairly common fault with the Canberra. The starter motor on the Avon engine which the Canberra has, is a device which fires a large pyrotechnic cartridge, the hot gas from this cartridge rotates the engine up to speed and it starts. This method of starting creates a lot of smoke and it's fairly common for the ignition points on the firing device to become covered with carbon and cease to function on the next start. The fix, clean off the ignition points. I knew this and I was pretty sure the young ground engineer did not, I was not keen on enlightening him. We consoled him with the fact that we were in no hurry at all, he could take all the time in the world to fix things, the more the better. In the meantime perhaps, as the local RAF representative, he could check us into the Lake Victoria Hotel, a place I had noticed on my previous visit to Entebbe with 24 Squadron, and do make sure they understand the RAF will be taking care of the bill, via East African Airways, BOAC, etc, I would be out of the Air Force and back in New Zealand before this one came home to roost. Well what a smart idea, the Lake Victoria Hotel was an exotic spot right on the equator, high up in the centre of Africa on the edge of a beautiful lake. It was the sort of resort where the rich and famous came to get away from it all, and had prices to match. Just make sure our representative has established the fact that East African Airways will be picking up the tab. Here we were in this place, three RAF jet jocks, with their own warplane, in an exclusive holiday resort with the rich and famous in the centre of Africa. We spent three days at the Lake Victoria Hotel, boy was it nice. We ate extremely well, no expense spared, it got to the stage where the French chef would come to our table in full chef's gear big hat and all, to have a glass of champagne with the *jet pilots*. We swam in the lake, it was delightful, then one evening in the bar I got talking with a hard case South African businessman who was drinking scotch and soda. I commented on the fact that scotch connoisseurs usually have water with their scotch, his response, 'not here young fellow, that's death.' 'Oh, how's that?' 'Bilharzia my boy, it will kill you.' 'Really, what's Bilharzia?' 'You don't know about it, dear me, let me give you some advice; never, never touch the water in these parts, not even to clean your teeth, if you do, then it's Bilharzia for you.' 'Really, well we were swimming in the lake today, is that ok?' 'No laddie that's not ok, that's Bilharzia.' This fellow was really starting to spoil my evening, 'tell me, what's going to happen to me because I swam in the lake?' Bilharzia is a water borne parasitic disease that gets into the body's bloodstream and causes problems, it can easily penetrate the unbroken skin, hence the problem with swimming in the lake. Drinking infected water is a surefire method of contracting it, hence my South African friend having soda with his scotch. 'Even the ice blocks are dangerous laddie, and I clean my teeth with soda water.' Well that's me gone, my life expectancy had just been shot to hell. Ever since that encounter I have looked at myself, have I or haven't I. I guess we were lucky, as far as I know none of us contracted Bilharzia.

We went into the local town Kampala one day and purchased some woodcarvings, all very African, I still have some of them. Bananas were a staple crop in this part of the world, really big bananas, they came in huge bunches about six feet long straight off the tree. It occurred to us that we could take some of these back to Germany, they would be a real novelty. There was a large metal mesh pannier in the Canberra bomb bay that was used for carrying things; like bananas. At cruising height the temperature in the bomb bay would be close to freezing so bananas should survive the trip back to Geilenkirchen, that would be when we were ready to leave, something we were actively trying to delay. Our holiday in Central Africa eventually came to an end. An engineer turned up from Nairobi who knew about Canberras, he would fix the starting problem and we would be on our way. We loaded the bomb bay with several huge bunches of bananas and were off. We transited Khartoum, and headed for Luqa in Malta, around the corner of Egypt, did not want to make waves, then fate stepped in. We developed another hydraulic problem and diverted into El Adem. It seemed I was always destined to visit El Adem whenever I headed for Africa. The problem was quickly fixed. We took off again and arrived at Luqa late at night, it had been a long day, eight hours strapped in a bang seat. The next day we flew to Geilenkirchen. For the next week or so everyone, including all our German friends, ate bananas.

A few years later I recall seeing the Lake Victoria Hotel in some news shots about Idi Amin. He had taken over the place and was using it as his own personal house. I shudder to think about what must have been going on there at that time. It was such a lovely spot when we visited in early 1963. Again I remember more news footage about the Israelis raiding Entebbe airport to rescue their citizens who had been hijacked by Arab extremists. It seems hard to comprehend how such a beautiful and peaceful place could descend into sheer terror.

I have often thought about that period in my life when I found myself in deepest darkest Africa doing Her Majesty's duty, gunboat diplomacy really, the sort of thing Empires are built on, but to me at the time nothing could be further from my mind, I was just having a good time, a great time. Hindsight's a wonderful thing. I often reflect on the fact that of all those fascinating places that we visited in our Canberra, most of them turned to custard just a few years later, Cyprus, Libya, Khartoum in the Sudan, Aden, Nairobi, Salisbury, Entebbe, not exactly tourist destinations today.

Final Days

Late in 1961 I met a young lady, a German citizen, who eventually became my wife. She had led an interesting life, born in Berlin at the height of the war, fleeing to Sweden with her family from East Germany then moving to South Africa. Becoming a fashion model there, then returning to Germany where we met and not long after that became engaged.

In the summer of 1962 I managed to get some time off and we both went south in the TR3 for a holiday. It was such an enjoyable time, let me tell you a little about it. We drove to Nice in the south of France then along the coast to Monte Carlo where we spent a few days. Monte Carlo was impressive, the signs of real wealth were all around, the cars in particular, they were all quite exotic expensive ones. We did not feel too bad, we were zipping around in this trendy English sports model, top down, attractive girl aboard, we thought we fitted in rather well. Then there was the Casino, that was a different story. One look at the cars parked outside and it was apparent that we were a little out of our league there, Rolls Royces, Maseratis, Ferraris, not a TR3 in sight, there was a dress code as well, tuxedos for the men, ball gowns for the ladies, then I found out that you had to prove your credit worthiness as well, that definitely ruled us out, I only had small change in my pocket. It was an incredible experience however, the first time I had seen the trappings of serious wealth. We were staying at a small pensione in Monte Carlo and surprisingly it was reasonably priced. I managed to borrow a camera from our host, silly me, did not have a camera. Ute and I went down to the Monte Carlo swimming pool which was an Olympic size affair set into the boat harbour amongst all the super yachts. I took some photos of Ute around the pool, remember this girl was a model, when she did the posing thing it was quite a sight. This attracted some attention amongst the locals and made us feel good, but I still only had small change in my pocket. We drove further along the coast, through San Remo, then to a beach resort in Italy called Varigotti. We checked into a small hotel right on the beach and enjoyed a few memorable days just lying on the sand in the sun, drinking wine, eating and eating very well. One thing that I thought was a bit different, all the beach umbrellas and sun lounges were lined up in neat rows on the sand, the rules were don't move them, then there was the Chianti. As I have frequently mentioned, being an RAF pilot did not make you wealthy. An incredibly good life style, a lot of fun, but not much ready cash. To stretch the available finances we investigated the lesser priced wines and this led us to the local Chianti. It came in a large fat bottle with the lower part enclosed in wickerwork, not a bad drop either. Then one day there we were sitting in the sun enjoying a bottle of this not too bad Chianti on this glorious Italian beach when suddenly the gloss went right off it all. Upending the bottle to extract the last few drops produced a whole lot of 'dark stuff' and some whole grapes. I guess that's what the wickerwork was meant to hide. From Varigotti we drove across the top of Italy to Venice. We spent three days there, were serenaded on a Gondola, visited some glassware factories, and enjoyed some fine food. Then it was north, through the Dolomites, very spectacular, and back into Germany. We were away for two weeks, that's all the time I could get off from the Cold War; it was a memorable holiday.

In October 1962 a situation that became known as the Cuban Missile Crisis developed. The Russians positioned ballistic missiles in Cuba, a tense standoff developed between America's President Kennedy, and Russia's Khrushchev. History tells us the world came perilously close to nuclear war, the Doomsday Clock was approaching midnight again. For 3 Squadron it meant a heightened state of alert and more LABS at Nordhorn. Cuba was a long way from Geilenkirchen. The events that unfolded there did not really impact on us as directly as the Berlin crisis the previous year. There was, however, a marked increase in our preparation for the real thing.

My time in the RAF was coming to an end. When I joined way back in 1955 the contract was for twelve years. During that time I could elect to make a career in the RAF or I could exercise an option to leave after eight, I elected to take the early leaving option. Shock, horror, nobody gives up such a good life after eight years, you should seriously consider a permanent commission, make a career of it, *'you're the right stuff,'* nope, not me, I fancy flying big jets around the Pacific and oh yes, the other thing, I'm tired of always being broke.

Shortly after the Entebbe interlude it came home to me that I was indeed about to leave the RAF, my days were numbered. A bit of nostalgia was creeping in, I also realised that the Queen would want her watch back, excuse me, what watch? When you become a pilot in the RAF you are issued with a very large Omega watch. The story is that you need this for navigation purposes, however, in reality it becomes just the watch that you wear all the time. It was a good watch, kept excellent time, but it was very big, the butt of numerous jokes. About all it really did, apart from telling the time to the very second, was to wear out the pocket on the left side of all your trousers. Well I was going to be without a watch, problem, where can I get a watch for my impending career change. They sell good watches cheap in Gibraltar. 'Sir, as I am about to leave the Air Force perhaps you could see your way clear to authorise a Southern Ranger to Gibraltar as a sort of parting thank you for being such a good squadron pilot for the past three years; and is that another gin and tonic sir?'

On February 7th 1963 myself and Tom Stonor set off for Gibraltar on what turned out to be my swansong in the RAF. I do not recall why Harry was not with us, I think he may have been on leave at the time. To give the trip some operational value we first flew to Luqa in Malta then the next day we flew a low level sortie over Libya returning to Luqa at the end of it. This sortie over Libya was fascinating. Prior to this, although we had spent a lot of time flying in Libya during our frequent visits to Idris, it had all been associated with bombing at Tarhunah, we had never really been able to go off and do a bit of low flying out over the desert. We flew inland from the coast, the endless desert panorama that opened up was quite amazing. All sand, there were areas where there were a lot of old wrecked vehicles and plenty of tracks in the sand, we later learned that it was debris left over from the Second World War. There had been a lot of fighting in the area, this was where Germany's Africa Corps had fought the British 8th Army, some monumental battles had been fought in this sandy wasteland. The desert, when observed from a low flying aircraft, and we were really low, was fascinating, there were hills and valleys in the sand, the occasional outcrop of rock, little sign of life, and absolutely no vegetation. We thundered around at low level for quite a while then climbed up to altitude and returned to Luqa, it had been an exhilarating experience. The following day was free. We spent an enjoyable interlude at the swimming club re-acquainting ourselves with prawns piri piri. On day four we flew to Gibraltar. I was looking for a watch, Tom was looking at diamonds, hang on Tom, your fiancée is in Rhodesia the diamond capital of the world. 'I know,' was Tom's response, 'but this is something that I have to do myself.' 'Ok but if it was me I think I would be chasing around Rhodesia.' I never did find out what Tom did in the end, he was very secretive on that one. Myself, I purchased a very fine Girard-Perregaux watch for my new life in civvy street, it was a good one and served me well for the next twenty years. The price was right too, that's the actual cost to me was right, the cost of flying a personal jet around the Mediterranean to make the purchase was not considered. That evening we went across the Spanish border to the local town, La Linea. Well Tom, and some English lads went across, me, well my New Zealand passport did not work at the border for some reason, help me fellows. Tom, who had a way with words, managed to convince the Spanish Border people that I was a visiting dignitary from New Zealand, a border crossing refusal would not be looked upon favourably by the British authorities in Gibraltar, good one Tom, I was across. Perhaps I should mention here that Tom stayed in the RAF and rose to the rank of Air Marshall. Off we went to Dirty Dick's, a legendary bar in La Linea where the idea was to 'drink the line.' Dick, or as he was known, Dirty Dick, was a larger than life character. The story goes he had got offside with Franco during the Spanish Civil War and been sentenced to a lifetime of internal detention. That meant he could not leave La Linea so he opened a bar, the 'world will come to me,' and it did. The bar in Dirty Dick's was a very long affair, there was a line of bar stools that went with it and a Flamenco Guitarist playing at one end. Set into the wall behind the bar were the ends of numerous wine casks, each with a spigot attached. Each cask contained a different wine, they were all cheap, just a few pesetas for a glass. The idea was to drink your way along the wall, if you survived then you could drink your way back again, well we did enjoy ourselves. Eventually the English Officers, and their VIP guest from New Zealand, staggered back across the border and into the local nightclub in Gibraltar. This club was renowned for its Flamenco dancers, I still clearly remember the brilliant demonstration of Flamenco dancing laid on just for us.

Next morning we were to fly back to Geilenkirchen, I had my watch, not sure about Tom's diamond, we were not in the best of health. The weather forecast did not help, large swaths of Northern

Europe were fogged in. Off we went, not long into the flight the weather over Northern Europe socked right in, Geilenkirchen went out in fog. Not much point in continuing, where will we divert too? At the time we were approaching the coast of Southern France, there's a large military airfield at Orange, which was quite close, we made radio contact and diverted into Orange. Fortuitously the keen young French Air Force Officer who greeted us was of the opinion that the French Officers Mess at Orange would not be up to the standard required for RAF Officers, 'really, what would you suggest?' 'I think you should be accommodated in a hotel in nearby Avignon.' 'Ok, if you insist.' Good move, Avignon is in the Rhone River valley, burgundy country, one of France's best red wine growing areas. The Chateauneuf-du-Pape winery, one of the very best, was close by. Well did we enjoy our stay, the food was superb and there was an endless supply of good red wine. The weather remained socked in over Northern Europe for another three days, we remained in Avignon, life was complete, and I was about to give it all up and go off to the South Seas.

On day three there was some clearance in the weather over Germany. We received a phone call from a worried boss at Geilenkirchen, he had not been able to get much information from the French about our circumstances. We assured him our circumstances could not be better and to stop worrying. Unfortunately the boss wanted the aeroplane back, he was having trouble keeping the squadron's alert status up to scratch. He told us the weather was still poor however he would like us to make an attempt to return. Damn, better do as we are told. Off we went but it was not good, Geilenkirchen still out in fog, we finished up at Laarbruch, an RAF airfield further to the north in Germany. We abandoned our aircraft at Laarbruch and travelled back to Geilenkirchen by road, the weather remaining socked in.

At times our B(I)8 flying took us far away from Geilenkirchen, we flew in conditions that varied in the extreme. One day we could be carrying out a strike in a Norwegian fjord in amongst the mountains, snow and ice all around, in weather that could vary from fine and clear to heavy overcast which would enclose the mountaintops and make the exercise quite spooky, a couple of days later we could be out in the Libyan desert, heat, sand, dust and flies, trying our best to toss a few small bombs into a 'pickle barrel' or we could be flying around Germany, or nearby France, right down on the deck on a murky day where the visibility was terrible, or a bright sunny one where you could see for miles. We could be doing some air to ground gunnery along the south coast of sunny Cyprus or flying over the vast plains of East Africa. We could be carrying out a high low high at night way up into Scotland or flying over the endless deserts of North Africa, or we could be drinking fine red wine in Avignon, we really did get around, it was just fantastic.

During March 1963, Harry and I did, what was for me, my last two flights with the RAF, they were both low level blasts through the low flying areas in northern Germany. There was a final dining in at Geilenkirchen for both Harry and I and suddenly it was all over. I was 26 years old, had just married, and had just enjoyed eight glorious years of flying, the last part of it in what was probably the best flying role in the RAF. It was an emotional time, Harry and I had been flying together for three years, we had shared some incredible experiences, some enjoyable, others downright terrifying. Harry looked quite a bit older than when I had met him at Bassingbourn, a few grey hairs were starting to appear, I guess you could put some of that down to what I had subjected him to from time to time during those years, all those LABS manoeuvres in particular. We shook hands, parted, and never saw each other again for forty-five years. Harry remained in the RAF, he became a navigator in the V Force, the RAF's heavy bomber Force, what did I do? well that's another story. I was off back to New Zealand, newly married, with a rather worn Triumph TR3A sports car, British racing green of course, a bank overdraft and the promise of an airline job, or so I thought! My days as a *Cold War Warrior* were over, I was off to the South Seas to follow more peaceful pursuits, the Big OE had come to an end, it had been an incredible experience.

Reflections

What effect did the Air Force have on me? Well I grew up very quickly. It started with the initial flying course in New Zealand, not for the faint hearted, the high attrition rate testifies to that; the unexpected death of my father followed by my departure for England and a very different environment. In the space of a few short years I changed from being a rather naïve youth from a rural backwater in New Zealand, to being the sole pilot of a high tech warplane capable of unleashing appalling nuclear destruction on Eastern Europe. I had been around the world before I was twenty-one, experienced things and been to places that I would never even have dreamed about. Did it all affect me? Of course it did! The two years with 24 Squadron and the three years at Geilenkirchen, had a huge impact on my life. I was witness to, been part of, momentous events that shaped the world for years to come. The full impact of what I was part of has only really sunk in years later when history has analysed just what went on in the world during that period and I had been an integral part of it all.

I guess I must have learnt how to deal with stress as well, particularly while I was at Geilenkirchen. I am not aware of any particular ability that I may have developed in this area except I have noticed during the latter part of my life that nothing seems to cause me too much concern. When I was at Geilenkirchen we did have two fellows who cracked up and were unable to continue flying, apparently the result of stress, but I don't really know. The flying in Germany never caused me any real problems, some frightening moments certainly, but then that was all part of the fun. I often wonder how my life would have turned out if certain things had worked out differently, the 'what ifs' of life. What if I had been able to take up that offer put forward by those two Cathay pilots on the tarmac at Labuan all those years ago? What if a shot had been fired during that tank confrontation at Checkpoint Charlie in Berlin in 1961, would I have got to walk on the beach at Bornholm or would I have perished in a huge fireball somewhere over Eastern Europe? What if we had been 'doing a Glennie' and were checking the pubs in East Berlin on that fateful Saturday night in August 1961 when the Berlin wall was started, perhaps the cracked ribs which laid me low and kept me home that evening, were meant to be. What if the STASI had nabbed me while I was wandering around East Berlin as we were allowed to do? And that taxi driver in Aden who took us to Crater? was it a set up? What if I had not found that hole in the cloud over El Adem that night? What if the French had got wind of what we were up to during that gun running episode? What if I had copped some radiation at Christmas Island, or, heaven forbid, had contracted Bilharzia at Entebbe? What if I had not done that trip to Geilenkirchen in the Hastings and seen those B(I)8s lined up on the tarmac? What if I had not accepted the offer made to me at Swinderby to do the Hastings course at Dishforth? and, what if I had screwed up on the wings course? I have often wondered if I would have been any good at architecture.

Mum was always worried she would never see me again, she never actually said it but I could tell. When I left her on the wharf in Wellington in 1956 and again when I went back to Germany in 1961, I think she thought that was the last she would ever see of me. I never told her but her fears were not without some foundation. I did not have a death wish, quite the opposite, however on several occasions at Geilenkirchen the Grim Reaper did reach out in my direction.

Just after I joined 59 Squadron I was taken up in the squadron T4, the instructor was an Australian chap, amongst other things he demonstrated a LABS manoeuvre. All new to me however I did not think that seeing the ground rushing up at a frightening speed, then being subjected to a huge G load which blacked me out followed by some expletives from my Australian instructor, was quite normal. It was not, he was very apologetic and also visibly shaken, he had screwed up. We had come as close as you would ever want to come to impacting the ground at high speed.

Then there was the loop incident in a B(I)8 at Nordhorn where I screwed up, Harry and I came perilously close to meeting our maker and all because of my mistake. That night over the North African coast when we got lost above cloud could have had dire consequences as could the Kiel Canal bridge episode. That close encounter with the White Cliffs of Dover could well have resulted in a black smudge on that famous landmark. We did not succumb to the Grim Reaper however, and Mum did not have her worst fears confirmed.

I did learn that you have to make things happen in your life, not wait around until someone else decides for you. I will be a pilot in the Royal Air Force, sorry Mum, I will be a jet jock, I will fly B(I)8s at Geilenkirchen and I will leave the Air Force, return to New Zealand, and fly big jets around the Pacific, that was how I progressively planned my life and that's what happened.

You may well be wondering how I recall all this, it's been many years since these events took place. Well pilots keep logbooks. I have a two volume log book, the first volume records all the flying I did in the Air Force. It's quite large and lives in a leather case up on the top shelf in the study. When I start looking at some of the entries it all comes flooding back, I lie awake at nights with the brain in overdrive and even more memories return. Then there are the letters. When I was well into this book I came across an old file that was amongst my mother's things that came into my possession when she passed away a few years ago. Dear old mum had transcribed all the letters that I had written home from Europe into type on her old typewriter and filed them away by month and year in this file. Typing them was a good idea, now they are quite easy to read. There are about eighty of them. Reading what I had written all those years ago is fascinating and brings back even more memories.

Medals, I don't have any. I often reflect on the fact that all the flying I was involved with was the sort that did not get publicity, not what medals are handed out for.

I fought the Cold War but I never got a medal.

My older brother Noel enjoyed a successful career as an opera singer, if you are interested in opera you may have heard of him. Unfortunately he succumbed to cancer some years ago. He made quite a name for himself in Europe. He was in Paris for several years then at Covent Garden during the 60s. Following that he spent many years as the resident bass at the Hamburg State Opera in Germany long after I had returned to New Zealand. I often reflect on just what the two Mangin brothers from far off New Zealand really contributed to European society. There was Noel deeply immersed in its cultural life, then there was me, thundering around in a noisy warplane making a nuisance of myself, intent on nuking the place. When Noel contracted cancer he returned to New Zealand and spent his final days here at our place in Howick where he eventually passed away. My dear old mum was still alive at the time, in her 90s, she idolised Noel. When he died she was completely devastated and passed away just eighteen months later.

During the whole time I was in the Air Force I did not have a camera. Photography just did not interest me, I have kicked myself ever since. I could have had some remarkable and historically very interesting pictures, hindsight is a wonderful thing. Christmas Island during the nuclear testing was a photographer's heaven and I do not have a single picture of my own. As for pictures of a B(I)8, unfortunately there were only a few B(I)8s made, there are not many photos around and I never took any at all.

When I returned to New Zealand I became involved in civil aviation, there's a book in the works about that. I was newly married and after a while Ute and I had a son, Peter. I am now a grandfather, I could well become a great grandfather. Sadly, after twenty years of marriage, Ute and I parted back in 1983, I now live with my partner Lynne, we have been together for the past thirty years.

During 2006 I started reflecting upon that time I spent in Europe, particularly Geilenkirchen, must be the approach of old age. I managed to make contact with Phil who still lives in England, then I managed to make contact with Harry as well, I suggested to them both that we must organise a get together of all the Geilenkirchen people from that period of our lives in the early 1960s. Time was marching on and if we did not do it sooner rather than later then we may not be doing it at all. It happened. In May 2007 Lynne and I travelled to England for a reunion with some of the people who had been at Geilenkirchen in Germany all those years ago. The get together we organised coincided with the 95th anniversary of No: 3 Squadron and the CO of the current 3 Squadron invited all the Geilenkirchen people to the 3 Squadron base at Coningsby in Lincolnshire. No:3 had just re-equipped with the brand new Typhoon Eurofighter, the very latest in fighter technology. We were given an extensive tour of the current facilities and let loose on the Typhoon simulator. Then we were guests at a flying display by some of the new aircraft including an incredible solo aerobatics display by one of the squadron pilots. Coningsby is also home for the Battle of Britain Memorial Flight and we were further treated to an inspection tour of their aircraft, five Spitfires, five Hurricanes, and a Lancaster, all currently airworthy. We were split up into small groups for this tour and given individual escorts, young fellows who were current 3 Sqdn Typhoon pilots. Our escort was a young lad in a flying suit, and I mean young, he looked like a schoolboy. We ribbed him about whether they only let him out from school to fly Typhoons at the

Typhoon - 2007

weekends. Since that memorable visit to Coningsby I have thought a lot about the past, I guess I must have looked a bit like that young bullet proof lad when I was at Geilenkirchen. Later in the day we were privileged to have a fly past laid on by the BBMF, as the memorial flight is known, just for us; a Lancaster flanked by a Spitfire and a Hurricane. We felt quite honoured.

Something that impressed me at Coningsby was the mental state of preparedness now required by the modern pilot to enable him to cope with the current state of the art combat aircraft. The simulator is now an essential piece of equipment constantly being used, pilots have to be right up to speed before they are allowed to fly the actual aircraft. When the squadron is detached elsewhere, and at that time the rumour was they were about to be detached to Afghanistan, they took along a portable simulator, all the pilots were required to fly it.

I might mention here that the modern jet fighter simulator is a rather different machine to what you might imagine. Gone are the huge

2007 - If Only

hydraulic jacks holding up a capsule that moves about. Now days the simulator is quite small, all the effects of flight are achieved by visual sensation, Actual combat situations can be simulated and a pilot's abilities in that area readily assessed. We were treated to a session in the Typhoon simulator, I was impressed. The impending Squadron detachment to Afghanistan, which was rather unusual for a high performance fighter squadron, was apparently to find out just how the Typhoon would perform in a desert environment. It was also intended to develop a ground attack version of the aircraft; well now, there you go, the Geilenkirchen fellows could give you plenty of advice there.

On the Saturday evening, May 12th 2007, we had a dinner for the

Geilenkirchen group at the Admiral Rodney Hotel in Horncastle, Lincolnshire, there were ten of us, our first get together for 45years, it was the last time I was to see Harry Scarff.

Old Warriors

Whatever happened to those magnificent B(I)8s that we had such a wonderful time flying? Well there were very few of them to start with, just three squadrons in service with the RAF, all in Germany. Nos: 3, 16, and 88. There would not have been more than about forty of them altogether. They continued on in the nuclear strike role for a further nine years after I left the scene then they were all withdrawn from service. What happened then? Well it's a sorry story really. Obsolete military aircraft have no value, especially larger jet ones. The various vintage aircraft organisations that are so prevalent today had not really appeared at that time. The B(I)8s were farmed out to various aviation fire fighting services so that the fire fighters could practise their skills, broken up for scrap, or just parked in fields to rot; some lucky ones were given to various aviation museums. A few were rebuilt, upgraded, and sold to various foreign Air Forces. But I think the ultimate disgrace was bestowed on a couple that were towed up to Nordhorn, the place where we used to shoot up everything and do a lot of bombing; they were used as gunnery targets for a later generation of ground attack aircraft. There are no B(I)8s left flying in the world today.

Recently the following information came to my attention. It relates to the demise of a No:3 Squadron B(I)8 in Germany in 1967, four years after I left the Squadron, the circumstances surrounding the crash resulted in the pilot being awarded the Air Force Cross, it also vividly describes just how difficult it could be to abandon a doomed B(I)8 as I have detailed elsewhere in this book.

The Queen has been graciously pleased to approve the award of the Air Force Cross to Flight Lieutenant R G Ledwidge, Royal Air Force. On the morning of 9th May 1967, Flight Lieutenant Ledwidge as pilot and captain of a Canberra was flying with his navigator on a low-level navigation and bombing training mission over Northern Germany. The major part of the flight had been successfully completed and the aircraft was returning to its base when, at a height of 500 feet above ground level, the aileron control suddenly jammed at about half left aileron deflection. The aircraft immediately started rolling onto its back. Realizing that his aircraft was in imminent danger Flight Lieutenant Ledwidge could at this point have used his ejector seat to escape, however he was aware that his navigator, who was not equipped with an ejector seat, would have no chance of escaping from the aircraft before it crashed. With complete disregard for his own safety, Flight Lieutenant Ledwidge attempted to regain partial control of the aircraft and, although he could not prevent it from continuing to roll, he was able, by a superb display of airmanship and piloting skill, to use differential engine power, rudder and elevator to prevent the aircraft from striking the ground during the first complete roll at low level. He then continued to control the aircraft through a series of full power climbing rolls, by using rudder to influence the rate of roll at different stages and thus gain as much height as possible during each manoeuvre. Flight Lieutenant Ledwidge had warned his navigator of the emergency immediately but the harsh use of the controls and the reversals of 'G' during the early stages of recovery had caused the navigator to become disconnected from the inter-communication system and be thrown around the aircraft cabin. It was not until the aircraft was climbing that the navigator was able to re-establish contact with the pilot, who instructed him to prepare to abandon. Flight Lieutenant Ledwidge then waited until the navigator had fitted his parachute pack and the aircraft was approaching the normal wings level attitude during one of the climbing rolls before giving the order to abandon the aircraft. Only when he had seen his navigator leave through the escape exit did he himself operate his ejector seat, by which time the aircraft had reached a height of about 8000 feet. Both the pilot and navigator made a successful descent by parachute and were quickly picked up by rescue services alerted by the distress call which the pilot radioed before abandoning the aircraft. Throughout the whole of the emergency, Flight Lieutenant Ledwidge displayed exceptional presence of mind. His handling of his aircraft in a dire emergency showed superior judgment and outstanding skill, determination, and sense of duty. These qualities, allied to a courage which is an example to all and in the very best traditions of a fighting service, undoubtedly saved his navigator's life.

The aircraft involved was XH204 the same aircraft Harry and I flew frequently during our time on No:3 Squadron including a lot of air to ground gunnery on the Larnaca range in Cyprus. It was sad to learn

XH204

that it ended up a smouldering pile of wreckage near the village of Wesel in Germany.

MIG 21

Our nemesis during the Cold War was a Soviet fighter that NATO codenamed Fishbed, the MIG 21, a formidable foe. These days, here in Auckland New Zealand, there is a real MIG 21 mounted on the roof of a factory in Penrose, an industrial suburb. It was purchased from the Polish Air Force many years ago by an aviation enthusiast and the idea was to get it flying here in New Zealand. This never

happened. It had several owners before eventually being mounted on this factory roof, it's certainly an arresting sight. Every time I drive by and see it, all the memories come flooding back. This particular aircraft could well have been my adversary if war had occurred in Europe, it belonged to the Polish Air Force: our target was in Poland.

Havelock School

When I was a young fellow in Blenheim there was a period when we went and lived at Mary's place in Havelock for a couple of months during a move between farms that Dad was managing. I was going to Blenheim primary school at the time. To maintain continuity I commuted daily on the bus, the smelly dusty bus, from Havelock, opportunity missed. If I had attended school in Havelock during this short period then perhaps my whole life would have been different; really? Havelock primary school produced two very famous people, Sir Ernest Rutherford, the man who split the atom and Sir William Pickering who headed up California's Jet Propulsion Laboratory, responsible for putting a man on the moon; perhaps there was something in the water there. My life could have taken a very different course, I might have been famous if only I had attended the Havelock school instead of enduring that smelly dusty bus for a couple of months. There is a connection, Uncle Doug was a Pickering.

White's Farm

That place of happy childhood memories, it's still there virtually unchanged. A while back we went down to Blenheim, I still have relatives there, on this occasion I made a point of seeking out White's farm and having a look, what a surprise, there it was nestled amongst the big old macrocarpa trees. It's been more than seventy years, the trees are very big. The old house is much the same, very run down, a little tree enclosed enclave surrounded my lush vineyards, the old sunburnt paddocks long gone. We crossed that 'bridge' I built with Dad and went up the long dirt track to the house. An old chap came out, I explained the reason for my visit, he was really interested. I told him how I lived in the house when I was six years old along with the wandering chooks, pigs, sheep and guess what, nothing's changed, it was like being in a time warp. The old chap was fascinated by my tale and showed me around. There had been some changes but the place was pretty much as I remembered it. It was fortunate we visited when we did, it was all about to disappear, the place had been sold, the land was just so valuable now. The house was going, the macrocarpa trees, the remnants of the outhouses where the chooks, the pigs and the sheep had lived, all about to disappear, to be replaced by neat rows of grape vines just like the surrounding area. The grape totally dominates Marlborough as far as the eye can see, it's now a very different place. Sunburnt paddocks, nodding thistle, gum trees, stony ground, scrawny cattle, miserable looking sheep, useless land, poor farmers, all gone: treasure the memories.

Harry's Death

A few days after returning from the trip to England in 2007 I received an e-mail from Harry's daughter in law that really shook me up; Harry had unexpectedly passed away. She was aware I was a close friend but she did not know how to contact me in far off New Zealand. Rummaging through Harry's things produced an e-mail address so an e-mail it was, the worst e-mail I have ever received. Apparently Harry had undergone some minor surgery to a leg and died under the anaesthetic. Life can produce some unexpected shocks at times.

It was shortly after Harry's death that I got the call from his son about the copper tankard. I now know that Harry's family still have one of the tankards we brought back from Rhodesia in 1962 and which the fellow in Geilenkirchen village did such a rough job engraving, I hope Gordon's family still have the third one.

So there you have it, the story about the copper tankard in the glass cabinet that's a constant reminder about my days as a *Cold War Warrior*.

Glossary

Airbrakes: A device that extends out into the airflow around the aircraft disrupting it and creating drag that slows the aircraft down.

Bang seat/Ejection seat: A seat that can be ejected from an aircraft with the pilot still strapped into it.

Blacked out: See a full explanation under *G* below.

Blue Silk Doppler: A self contained radar navigation system based on the Doppler principle which at the time was quite an advance on what had been available for military aircraft. Blue Silk was remarkably accurate. It had been developed specifically for high flying nuclear bombers. It enabled our B(I)8s to operate quite independently of any ground based navigation aids when we were at altitude which was not very often.

Circuit/base leg: Two terms used to describe just where, in relation to an airfield, an aircraft is positioned when it is coming in to land. 'In the circuit' means that the aircraft is usually 1000 feet above the ground flying a roughly rectangular pattern around the airfield. 'Base leg' is the last bit of the circuit just before the aircraft makes the final turn to line up with the runway.

Cockpit Canopy: The original Canberra design included a rather restrictive bubble canopy for the pilot. The B(I)8 had a fighter style canopy that gave the pilot a much improved field of view, pretty essential when you consider the type of flying that the B(I)8s were doing.

Cold War: A forty year period, from the late 1940s, until the collapse of the Soviet Union in 1991. The Western Powers, led by America, confronted the Eastern Bloc countries, led by the Soviet

Union. Both sides built up huge armed forces, the potential for catastrophic nuclear conflict was very real.

Elevator: The moving control surface attached to the rear of the tailplane that allows the aircraft to be manoeuvred up or down.

Flash bomb: A small twenty-five pound bomb widely used in the military for practise purposes. When it strikes the ground it fires a small charge which gives out a bright flash that enables an observer to see just where the bomb has struck.

Flick Stall: A condition where one wing stalls slightly before the other one and the aircraft rolls rapidly towards the stalled wing, or flicks.

Head up instrument display: When a pilot is flying along and looking outside his eyes are focused at infinity. When he looks inside to check his instruments he refocuses his eyes. If you do this while flying fast and low then something may suddenly appear outside that you may miss because you are focused inside at the time. To overcome this problem a system called a head up display was developed which projects the essential flight instrument readings onto the windscreen directly in front of the pilot and focused at infinity. This allows the pilot to continue looking outside, with his eyes focused at infinity and have the flight instruments in his field of view at the same time.

Under the hood: Pilots are trained to be able to fly solely on the flight instruments alone without any external visual reference. To enable this to be practised a hood is placed around the trainee pilot's head so that he is unable to see outside the aircraft.

G: The force of gravity. On the Earth's surface everything is subjected to a downward force of 1G, this determines the weight of everything. In an aeroplane the pilot can pull back on the control column and make the aeroplane go upwards, or accelerate up, this will effectively increase the weight of the aeroplane and its contents. This will be felt by a pilot as an increase in the force pulling him downwards, or an increase in G. Taken to the extreme it will cause a draining of blood from the brain resulting in unconsciousness, or black out.

Javelin: An all weather night fighter made by the Gloster Aircraft Company in England, widely used by the RAF during the 1950s and 60s. It was a little unusual in that it had a delta wing configuration which was a radical departure from previous fighter aircraft design.

Megaton: The explosive equivalent of one million tons of TNT.

MIG: A Russian fighter aircraft widely used by the Eastern Bloc countries and some Arab air forces.

NATO: North Atlantic Treaty Organisation.

Nuke: Short for nuclear weapon.

Socked in: A slang expression meaning the visibility is very poor.

Spin: The aircraft has stalled, dropped a wing and entered a spiral dive with the wings remaining in a stalled condition.

Stall: Basically a condition where an aeroplane ceases to fly and falls out of the sky. When the airflow over an aircraft's wing is disrupted to such an extent that no lift is produced then the aircraft stalls. Usually a stall occurs when an aircraft's speed becomes too slow however a stall can occur at high speed if too much G is pulled. When this happens the angle of attack, that is the angle at which the wing meets the airflow over it, is increased too much and the smooth airflow over the wing breaks down.

Tactical nuke: A nuclear weapon used in a close support role that will have an immediate effect on the current battle.

Tailplane: The 'mini wing' at the rear of the aeroplane.

TNT: Trinitrotoluene. A high explosive that is widely used as a yardstick for measuring the power of other explosives.

Topple: The artificial horizon is a large instrument located in the centre of the pilot's instrument panel and represents the earth below and the sky above much the same as looking outside the aircraft. The pilot can fly along, correctly orientated, by just using this one instrument. When the aircraft pulls up into a loop then at the top of the loop when the aircraft is upside down the artificial horizon will be indicating incorrectly, the earth and the sky will be reversed. When this happens most artificial horizons will topple which means that the gyro that controls the instrument goes out of control and the instrument is no longer usable. In our B(I)8s we had an advanced instrument which, at the top of the loop, when we were upside down, would rotate through 180 degrees to again give a correct presentation, ground below and sky above. This allowed us to rollout using the artificial horizon as the sole reference.

About the Author

Rex Mangin, and his partner Lynne, live in a cottage on a beach in Auckland, New Zealand. He spends his time doing up the cottage, writing, fishing, and travelling. He is planning another couple of books about what he got up to after leaving Germany.

Back In The Mediterranean In More Recent Years.

Books By Rex Mangin

These books by Rex Mangin are available as paperbacks and at all e-book outlets worldwide.

Infidelity Gun Running & Other Tales

Fourteen short stories drawn from the author's vast treasure trove of experiences. He spent a lifetime in aviation, both military and civilian, became involved in the Cold War in Europe, nuclear testing at Christmas Island, topdressing in New Zealand, and spent many years flying the Pacific. Now retired, he has turned his hand to writing. His aviation background is reflected in many of these stories.

Set in Europe, North Africa, Hong Kong, New Zealand. Sydney, Honolulu, Christmas Island, Tahiti, Mo'orea, Rangiroa, and Bora Bora, it's a diverse and entertaining collection of fact and fiction, all based on the author's real-life experiences.

The dramatic engine failure described in *A Close Call In Tahiti* did occur, July 17th 1980, at Faa'a Airport in Papeete. The *Gun Running* happened back in 1957.

The author flew into Hong Kong's old Kai Tak airport many times. *Remember Kai Tak* describes just what it was like flying into that extraordinary place. The yacht featured in *Andria* is the *Jardilinka*, a well-known vessel in Hong Kong waters. The author was lucky enough to enjoy many cruises on this fine old vessel.

The Jury is a true story as are *A Curious Business, The Bottle*, and *Christmas Island. A Labs Attack* describes some of the things that went on during the Cold War, all true, these things happened.

Aerial topdressing features in *The Greening Of Northland*, an insight into this unique New Zealand industry.

I'm sure you'll enjoy reading these stories just as much as the author enjoyed writing them.

Flying The Pacific (a memoir)

After several years in NATO's Second Tactical Air Force on the front line of the Cold War in Germany the author returned to his native New Zealand and joined TEAL, Tasman Empire Airways. During a thirty year career with the airline he was part of the enormous expansion into the present day Air New Zealand. He flew everything from the jet prop Electra to the 747-400. The Pacific, the Orient, America, and during the later part of his career all the way to Europe. It was not a simple process however, there was a lot of angst and heartache.

This book is not just about flying it includes everything else that's involved in an airline pilot's life, the travel, the 'holiday' stopovers, living abroad, interesting experiences, some of them very interesting, the stresses and pressures, the rewards, it's a rather unique lifestyle.

Here's a sample of the first chapter.

Joining TEAL

'Got the checkerboard?'

'Yep, got it,' replies the co-pilot.

'Height ok?' I ask.

'Yep, looking good.'

'Ok when that tall building with the mast over on the right is abeam we'll turn.'

'Yep it's coming up now.'

'That wind's picked up, better turn a fraction earlier' the co-
    pilot offers.
'Yep, thanks.'
'Right; go now.'

We are flying a DC8, it's Hong Kong's notorious checkerboard approach at the old Kai Tak airport. I bank the big jet steeply to the right and peer out looking for the runway, there it is, right on cue. It's a murky evening, there's a strong crosswind blowing us right into the checkerboard, it's bumpy and we're in amongst the tall buildings. This approach is one of the more challenging things in aviation, not for the faint hearted. There's a stiff southerly requiring the use of runway 13, the south easterly one and that necessitates the famous checkerboard approach, the one the passengers love, the one that takes you right in amongst the tall buildings. The downside is that when this approach is required there's always a stiff crosswind on the runway. We complete the turn onto finals, assess the crosswind, kick in some rudder and prepare for the actual touchdown still with quite a bit of drift on. Just before the wheels make contact I kick it straight; the touchdown is quite smooth. Hold the wing down, careful with the reverse that wind is strong. We decelerate and turn off the runway; another adrenaline fuelled Hong Kong arrival. How come I'm doing this? I'm 32 years of age and this is one of aviation's more difficult places to be flying and in a big jet full of people. It's quite a story.

Mercenary
(a novel)

Rex Macare, fresh out of the military, a highly qualified pilot, his apprenticeship's finished, now he wants the real money. His quest leads to the mysterious Mr Roberts who makes him an offer too good to refuse. He meets and falls in love with the beautiful Kate, a high end fashion model.

He soon finds himself immersed in a whole new world. A heady mix of big money, huge money, dangerous flying, high end fashion, and unbridled sex. It does not last.

The story is set around the world, the South Seas, Vietnam, Paris, Algeria, Australia, and the DDR, the German Democratic Republic, the old East Germany.

It's a fast moving story that I'm sure you will enjoy.

Mr Roberts

Bzzzz, I press the doorbell, 'Monsieur Robier?' no response, I knock, 'Monsieur Robier?' still no response, have I made a mistake. I'm sure it was two this afternoon, room 202. I push the door, it swings open and I recoil in horror. The place is a charnel house, blood everywhere. There's a body on the floor, throat slashed open, I feel faint, want to throw up, it's worse than a horror movie. I look closer, the body has been mutilated, clothing torn open, blood all over the place, it's Monsieur Robier. There's something on his chest, a note.

Rentrez chez vous Monsieur Rex, ne plaisante pas avec nous.

Go home Mister Rex, don't mess with us.

French, English, my name, it's meant for me, shit! There's something else, his genitals have been torn off and stuffed into his mouth, the FLN's brutal calling card.

Albert McConachie's Bad Day

A three part tale about the slow decline of Albert McConachie's matrimonial life into total disaster. Albert however, quite unexpectedly, finds love elsewhere. The three parts of this tale are interspersed with a collection of short stories that you will find entertaining and amusing. The trivial, amusing, disastrous, childhood memories that you can probably relate to.

Carrie Gray
(a novel)

A young girl leaves New Zealand for Europe, the big OE. She goes alone, wants do her own thing, unrestricted by others, experience everything. A skilled boaty she wants to crew on a superyacht; she disappears.

Her boyfriend, Michael, becomes concerned at the sudden lack of communication and sets off to find her; he disappears.

Michael's father Frank, a retired detective, becomes alarmed and sets off to find them both. He discovers a frightening underworld of drug smuggling, murder, and prostitution, dominated by several powerful families. It's devoured these two youngsters from far off New Zealand.

A fast moving story of romance, adventure, and danger set in Paris, Athens, and Istanbul, and spills out into the Pacific.

Travel Bites

'You're under arrest sir.'

'Excuse me?'

'You're under arrest.'

Excuse me indeed; how can this be? I was at the immigration desk at Los Angeles airport, just got off a big jet after flying all the way from Auckland, when I was confronted with this. *I was the Captain!*

A collection of short stories, all travel related. The author spent much of his life travelling the world, and accumulated a mother lode of experiences. Some of these are shared in this book.

9 798230 347958